Digital Transformation with Dataverse for Teams

Become a citizen developer and lead the digital transformation wave with Microsoft Teams and Power Platform

Srikumar Nair

BIRMINGHAM—MUMBAI

Digital Transformation with Dataverse for Teams

Group Product Manager: Pavan Ramchandani

Senior Editor: Hayden Edwards

Content Development Editor: Aamir Ahmed

Technical Editor: Joseph Aloocaran, Saurabh Kadave

Copy Editor: Safis Editing

Project Manager: Divij Kotian

Proofreader: Safis Editing

Indexer: Tejal Daruwale Soni

Production Designer: Nilesh Mohite

First published: September 2021
Production reference: 1290921

Published by Packt Publishing Ltd.
Livery Place
35 Livery Street
Birmingham
B3 2PB, UK.

ISBN 978-1-80056-648-4

www.packt.com

To the loving memory of my parents, Sridevi Nair and Krishnankutty Nair, for their sacrifices and exemplifying grit through all difficult times in life, which continues to inspire me every day to be my best self.

To my lovely wife, Neetu, for being a great partner and my pillar of support.

To my wonderful kids, Siddhesh and Nandini, who inspire and encourage me with their unbounded energy and relentless curiosity.

To my teachers, who nurtured my curiosity and passion for learning.

To my friends and family, who stood with me through all times.

To all the frontline COVID warriors around the world, who have sacrificed a lot during the ongoing COVID-19 pandemic to keep all of us safe.

- Srikumar Nair

Foreword

I have known Srikumar Nair for 4 years through our work together on building the Power Platform. As the Corporate Vice President of Business Applications and Platforms at Microsoft, I lead the development of the low-code/no-code Power Platform as well as the Dynamics 365 suite of business applications that power businesses across the world. For businesses in every industry and every geography on this planet to deliver on the surging need for digital transformation, we need to empower everyone to contribute to the effort. This is where low-code/no-code development comes in, and this book by Srikumar is a fantastic way to get started.

We are seeing unprecedented digital demand, with companies focusing on rapidly building digital-first, intelligent experiences. It is estimated that 500 million more apps will be created in the next 5 years, which is more than all the apps built in the last 40 years[1]. On the other hand, there are not enough developers to meet this need – in the United States alone, there is a developer shortfall of 1 million today.[2] To meet this demand, we need to equip everyone to be a developer. This is possible through low code, which empowers everyone – from citizen to professional developers and IT admins – to go faster.

This book introduces key concepts in Power Platform, and provides step-by-step tutorials on building, deploying, and managing your first app, bot, and flow. It also includes pointers to additional resources to help you continue to learn and grow your skills. It encapsulates not only how to build solutions to meet your organization's needs, but also how to secure and govern your business-critical data and resources. With this book, I am confident you will be equipped to begin your journey as a citizen developer.

Charles Lamanna
Corporate Vice President, Business Applications and Platforms,
Microsoft

References:

[1] IDC FutureScape: Worldwide IT Industry 2020 Predictions

[2] BLS, NSF, NCES, IDC, Gartner, LinkedIn, C+AI Corp Strat

Contributors

About the author

Srikumar Nair is a product management leader with 20 years of experience building new products and features and improving the efficiency of products such as operating systems and business/productivity applications. Being a mechanical engineer, he started his career in the manufacturing sector but later developed a flair for software and joined Infosys as a software engineering intern. He eventually graduated as a professional developer in Java and .NET and then turned toward product/technology management with Microsoft, working in Office 365, SharePoint Online, enterprise mobility, Dynamics 365, and Power Platform. He is currently working as the principal group program manager in the Microsoft Dataverse team, focusing on infrastructure provisioning at scale, licensing, and improving service efficiency.

I want to thank the following people who helped me immensely in converting the vision of this book into reality:

Group Product Manager: *Pavan Ramchandani, for reaching out to me with this proposal*

Senior Editor: *Hayden Edwards, for setting a high bar for content reviews throughout this book*

Content Development Editor: *Aamir Ahmed, for his thorough review and patience while working with me throughout the content development of this book*

Technical Reviewer: *Marc Mercuri, for taking time out of his busy schedule to provide technical input for various chapters in this book*

About the reviewer

Marc Mercuri led and launched Dataverse for Teams. Across close to two decades at Microsoft, he has held a number of product, strategy, and innovation roles. He has authored 4 books and has over 25 patents issued or pending.

Table of Contents

3

Building Your First App with Microsoft Dataverse for Teams

4

Enhancing Your App with Images, Screens, and File Attachments

Section 2: Deep Dive into Microsoft Dataverse for Teams

5

Understanding Microsoft Dataverse

6

Automating with Microsoft Dataverse for Teams

7

Building Power Virtual Agents Bots with Microsoft Dataverse for Teams

Section 3: Application and Environment Life Cycle Management

8

Managing the Application Life Cycle and Environment Life Cycle

9
Upgrading to Microsoft Dataverse Environment

Section 4: Enterprise Readiness and Licensing

10
Ensuring Enterprise Readiness: Security and Governance

11
Licensing for Microsoft Dataverse and Dataverse for Teams

Preface

Microsoft Dataverse for Teams is a built-in, low-code data platform for Teams that enables everyone to easily build and deploy apps, flows, and intelligent chatbots in Teams with Power Apps, Power Automate, and Power Virtual Agents (PVA).

This book provides a detailed insight into Microsoft Dataverse for Teams. You'll learn how to build apps with step-by-step explanations for setting up Teams, creating tables to store relational data, and setting up basic security roles. With the techniques covered in the book, you'll be able to develop your first app with Dataverse for Teams within an hour! You'll then learn how to automate background tasks or alerts using Power Automate and Power Virtual Agents. As you get to grips with building business applications, you'll also find out when to consider upgrading from Dataverse for Teams to Dataverse and how they differ. Finally, you'll explore features for administration and governance and understand the nuances of product licensing with Microsoft Dataverse for Teams and Power Apps.

Having acquired the skills to build and deploy an enterprise-grade app, by the end of this book, you'll have become a fully qualified citizen developer and will be ready to lead a digital revolution in your organization.

Who this book is for

The book is for citizen developers, business professionals, or anyone looking to develop applications to solve critical business problems. Basic knowledge of using software such as PowerPoint, Excel-like formulae, and navigating between application screens is all you need to get started with this book.

What this book covers

Chapter 1, Introducing Digital Transformation and the Role of Low-Code/No-Code Platform, is where we will take a quick look at the new trends that are impacting our personal and work lives (that is, the consumer world and business environments) and how every one of us needs to be prepared to leverage these changes in technology to our advantage.

Chapter 2, Exploring Microsoft Dataverse for Teams, is where you will learn more about **Microsoft Dataverse for Teams** and the various components of the **Power Platform**, which forms the foundation of this low-code/no-code platform experience within Microsoft Teams.

Chapter 3, Building Your First App with Microsoft Dataverse for Teams, is where you will build your first low-code/no-code application, **Health Scanner**, using Microsoft Dataverse. Such an application can be used to keep a record of the health statistics of employees or students before the beginning of a shift or lesson.

Chapter 4, Enhancing Your App with Images, Screens, and File Attachments, is where you will learn about some advanced topics of Dataverse, such as using versions, usage analytics, and leveraging images and attachments to enhance your application.

Chapter 5, Understanding Microsoft Dataverse, is where you will learn about the different components of Microsoft Dataverse's layers, as well as studying scenarios to consider for an upgrade from Dataverse for Teams to Dataverse.

Chapter 6, Automating with Microsoft Dataverse for Teams, is where you will learn how to automate business tasks using Power Automate Flow in our Health Scanner application.

Chapter 7, Building Power Virtual Agents Bots with Microsoft Dataverse for Teams, is where you will leverage the power of PVA in the Health Scanner application, by authoring a chatbot that will help answer end users' questions.

Chapter 8, Managing the Application Life Cycle and Environment Life Cycle, is where you will learn about the different types of environments, the administration experience for these environments, and life cycle management for these environments and applications within Microsoft Dataverse for Teams.

Chapter 9, Upgrading to Microsoft Dataverse Environment, is where you are going to see how to upgrade a Microsoft Dataverse for Teams environment into a standard Dataverse environment that can support standalone apps built using Power Apps, Power Automate flows, and PVA bots.

Chapter 10, Ensuring Enterprise Readiness: Security and Governance, is where you are going to learn about the security and governance concepts that are important in the Dataverse for Teams environment.

Chapter 11, Licensing for Microsoft Dataverse and Dataverse for Teams, is where you are going to learn about the licensing requirements for Dataverse for Teams and other Power Platform products.

To get the most out of this book

Here are the Microsoft 365 licenses with which you will be able to use Dataverse for Teams:

- Office 365 E1, E3, E5

- Microsoft 365 E1, E3, E5

- Microsoft 365 F1, F3, F5

Software/hardware covered in the book	Operating system requirements
Office 365 (E1, E3, or E5 license plans) Compare Office 365 Enterprise | Microsoft (`https://www.microsoft.com/en-us/microsoft-365/enterprise/compare-office-365-plans`)	
Supported browser for accessing Office 365: `https://support.microsoft.com/en-us/office/which-browsers-work-with-office-for-the-web-and-office-add-ins-ad1303e0-a318-47aa-b409-d3a5eb44e452`	Windows, macOS, or Linux

Download the color images

We also provide a PDF file that has color images of the screenshots and diagrams used in this book. You can download it here: `https://static.packt-cdn.com/downloads/9781800566484_ColorImages.pdf`.

Conventions used

There are a number of text conventions used throughout this book.

`Code in text`: Indicates code words in text, database table names, folder names, filenames, file extensions, pathnames, dummy URLs, user input, and Twitter handles. Here is an example:

```
Concatenate(NeedAttention.Selected.'First Name', " ",
NeedAttention.Selected.'Last Name')
```

Bold: Indicates a new term, an important word, or words that you see onscreen. For instance, words in menus or dialog boxes appear in **bold**. Here is an example: "Select **System info** from the **Administration** panel."

> **Tips or important notes**
> Appear like this.

Get in touch

Feedback from our readers is always welcome.

General feedback: If you have questions about any aspect of this book, email us at customercare@packtpub.com and mention the book title in the subject of your message.

Errata: Although we have taken every care to ensure the accuracy of our content, mistakes do happen. If you have found a mistake in this book, we would be grateful if you would report this to us. Please visit www.packtpub.com/support/errata and fill in the form.

Piracy: If you come across any illegal copies of our works in any form on the internet, we would be grateful if you would provide us with the location address or website name. Please contact us at copyright@packt.com with a link to the material.

If you are interested in becoming an author: If there is a topic that you have expertise in and you are interested in either writing or contributing to a book, please visit authors.packtpub.com.

Share Your Thoughts

Once you've read *Digital Tranformation with Dataverse for Teams*, we'd love to hear your thoughts! Scan the QR code below to go straight to the Amazon review page for this book and share your feedback.

https://packt.link/r/1-800-56648-4

Your review is important to us and the tech community and will help us make sure we're delivering excellent quality content.

Section 1: Introduction to Microsoft Dataverse for Teams

This section of the book introduces you to digital transformation and why it is essential for all organizations to go through it to survive. It also shows how low-code/no-code platforms have a critical role to play in bridging the gap created due to a shortage of the manpower that is needed to achieve digital transformation for all the organizations around the world. In this section, you will also be introduced to Microsoft Power Platform and Microsoft Dataverse for Teams as well as building your first low-code/no-code app.

This section comprises the following chapters:

- *Chapter 1, Introducing Digital Transformation and the Role of Low-Code/No-Code Platform*
- *Chapter 2, Exploring Microsoft Dataverse for Teams*
- *Chapter 3, Building Your First App with Microsoft Dataverse for Teams*
- *Chapter 4, Enhancing Your App with Images, Screens, and File Attachments*

1

Introducing Digital Transformation and the Role of Low-Code/No-Code Platform

This book will help you to develop an understanding of what digital transformation is and why it is important to each one of us. It will also introduce you to a low-code/no-code platform built into Microsoft Teams, and help you develop proficiency in solving challenges faced by your organizations in their journey to achieve digital transformation. This book is intended to be used by *anyone* who wishes to build apps, bots, and workflows, and who wants to help automate a lot of manual processes within their organization, whether they're a student, a teacher, an entrepreneur, a doctor, or even a volunteer at a non-profit organization. As you progress through the first couple of chapters in this book, you will realize that with very basic skills, such as creating formulas, and a basic understanding of how you want your screens to look, you will be building very effective digital solutions for your organization.

In this chapter, we will take a quick look at the new trends that are impacting our personal and work lives (that is, the consumer world and business environments) and how every one of us needs to be prepared to use these changes in technology to our advantage, especially in our professional careers.

This chapter also begins to introduce you to Power Platform and Microsoft Dataverse for Teams, which not only helps you to build apps, bots, and flows with minimum training, but also accelerates the pace of digital transformation within your organization. Microsoft Dataverse for Teams provides rich data storage for all types of data, along with enterprise-grade governance and security. You will be able to acquire apps and install them with one-click deployment, almost like downloading an app to your personal smartphone from an app store.

In this chapter, we will cover the following topics:

- Understanding Digital Evolution
- Digital Evolution in Organizations
- Digital Transformation
- Introducing Microsoft Power Platform

Understanding Digital Evolution

The twentieth century belonged to organizations that adopted rapid mechanization and industrialization, riding on the wave of the third industrial revolution. The World Wars accelerated the need for countries and organizations to benefit from this wave of industrialization. There were a few other waves that followed and defined the progress of digital and automation experiences, such as the evolution of personal computing, the increased reach of the internet and the dot.com wave, and the advent of smartphones. All these innovations helped organizations and individuals to redefine the boundaries of what can be achieved and how much can be achieved in a short space of time. While it may have addressed some of the short-term goals of digital reach and automation, the desire for a total transformation of business process and productivity continues to grow like never before.

Here is a chronology of some significant milestones in the evolution of digital technology and how these advances have improved automation levels in various aspects of our lives:

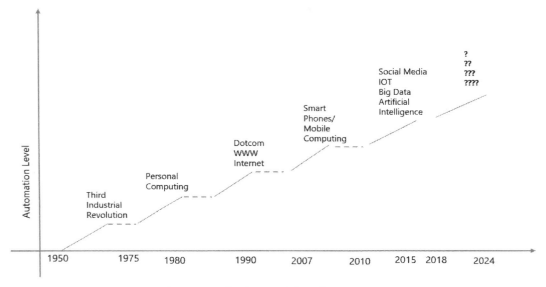

Figure 1.1 – Evolution of digital experience

On the consumer digital experience front, the last decade has seen a significant rise in mobile computing and hardware reducing in size to become personal wearables. The best evidence of this is the rising market for mobile computing devices. Even though the sale of such devices might have been impacted by the worldwide contraction of the economy owing to the COVID-19 pandemic, mobile phones still constitute more than 80% of the total devices market for 2020.

The consumer digital evolution is waiting to explode further with the wearables market, where personal healthcare data from millions of consumers will be monetized over the coming years. We have already seen the smartwatch industry boom, with Apple taking a large share of the market. Amazon has also announced its Halo Band, which claims to help customers to improve their health and wellness.

While there is much to study and analyze in the consumer digital evolution space, for the purpose of this book, we will focus on the digital evolution and transformation that is happening in enterprises and organizations.

Digital Evolution in Organizations

Organizations have realized the power of data – it is the new oil. Data is flowing in terabytes and petabytes per second, through social media and through **Internet of Things (IoT)** devices that are being wired to all living and non-living things on the planet. To give some examples, here are some of the top scenarios where organizations are using social media:

- Monitoring Twitter feeds for mentions and sentiment analysis, such as reactions based on negative tweets, and offering to resolve personal complaints

- Offering discounts and coupons to customers who "like" and promote the organization's brand

- Identifying and targeting a social group of customers for special campaigns based on location, age, social status, likes, search history, and so on

- Using professional networking sites such as LinkedIn feeds or Twitter ads to influence senior IT leaders and decision makers and generate leads for your business software or professional services that your organization offers

This demonstrates the evolution of marketing and customer service processes with the advent of social media, which helps organizations to improve their branding as well as improve their customer reach.

While this digital evolution continues, organizations need to be ready to harness the power of digital evolution to their advantage. Technology is not stagnant and keeps evolving as a byproduct of digital evolution. Who would have thought that one of the oldest industries, which delivers your daily pack or bottle of milk, would use 5G connected cows (https://www.reuters.com/article/us-telecoms-5g-cows/5g-connected-cows-test-milking-parlor-of-the-future-idUSKCN1RN1IY) to increase their output of premium quality milk? As you can see in this example, an industry where you wouldn't expect technology to make inroads is pioneering the latest technology to make operations more efficient, make products more desirable, and exceed customer expectations.

At this juncture, it is important to understand the digital transformation process in detail, which we will cover in the next section, along with why it is important for all organizations to not just survive but make large strides to thrive in the ever-emerging world of technology.

Digital Transformation

Digital transformation is the process of using advancements in technology to continuously evaluate and:

- *Empower employees*
- *Transform* products and services
- *Streamline* Operations
- *Exceed* customer expectations:

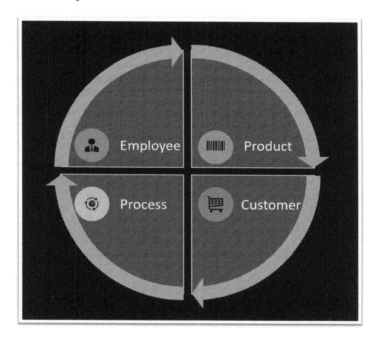

Figure 1.2 – Pillars of digital transformation

There are several definitions available on the internet, but the one that I mentioned here has the essence of what most organizations desire to do through their digital transformation endeavors.

Each of the pillars that form the bedrock of any digital transformation has significance, and one cannot be deemed more important than the other. However, depending on the maturity of the organization and market conditions, one of the pillars might need to be prioritized over the other by the organization's leaders.

One of the most challenging and crucial portions of this digital transformation is to energize and empower your workforce to not only participate but also lead and accelerate this transformation at grassroots level. Let's take a closer look at how employees can be empowered on this mission.

Empower employees

How do you empower employees of an organization to lead and accelerate the digital transformation journey? This empowerment comes from making employees contribute directly to the digital transformation and making them equal partners in celebrating the wins and dissecting the losses.

About 10-15 years ago, a frontline worker or information worker would at best be providing a set of requirements to the business analyst, who would then draft hundreds of pages of **Business Requirements Documents** (**BRDs**). These BRDs would then get passed on to the **Information Technology** (**IT**) department to build the next set or a new version of a **Line of Business** (**LOB**) application. LOB apps are built or procured from third-party vendors and their purpose is to solve typical business problems within an organization or within an industry. Examples include a talent management app for HR, invoice approval or tax calculation apps for finance, and an expense reporting app for all employees. During the building process, there will be various sub-phases of planning, design, development, and testing, before the application is ready for consumption. By the time the application is ready for production use, it is already too late, because the next version, and most of the ground assumptions and principles, would have changed or evolved, such as the number of users, scenarios, stakeholders, and business goals. There is a heavy price to be paid for this failure and, evidently, the pace of transformation suffers a great deal.

Another point worth noting is that millennials are a significant portion of the workforce today, and that percentage is going to increase in the upcoming years. What does this mean? This population is much more ambitious and technically literate, and they are going to be using technology both at work and in their personal lives. As part of engaging with this young and growing workforce every day, we realize that a majority of this new workforce is motivated to spend less time doing manual, labor-intensive, repetitive work and wants to focus more on adding value to the organization in much more meaningful ways. This is a favorable situation for organizations to have. It would be perilous for organizations to not have the right strategy, nor invest in the right set of technology to tap into this vast workforce and use them to transform their businesses.

Additionally, there is increased pressure for every one of us to start learning to code, including kids in school (https://www.nytimes.com/2017/06/27/technology/education-partovi-computer-science-coding-apple-microsoft.html). There are obvious benefits of learning to code, such as helping us to boost creativity and problem-solving abilities, and increasing professional advancement opportunities. However, it cannot be refuted that not everybody is wired to be an excellent coder and loves doing this all the time! It cannot be denied that some of the most creative minds in technology have not been the best or greatest coders, but they were always driven by their passion to innovate and make a change, a very good example being the legendary Steve Jobs. This book is going to be of immense help for such innovators who wouldn't like to spend a lot of time learning to code in a new language before bringing their ideas to fruition.

Anybody can build an app and automate without formal knowledge of coding; this is where the promise of this new low-code/no-code platform that is now available with Microsoft Teams and Microsoft Dataverse for Teams comes into play. This enables technology to meet people where they are, rather than asking them to go through a massive learning curve of learning to code in a certain language before deciding to solve a business problem. Thus, we will be empowering everyone to build low-code/no-code applications and other digital solutions to make a change, whether they are an information worker within an organization, a teacher in an elementary school, an analyst in an investment bank, a health professional in a hospital, a volunteer at a non-profit organization, or whoever. In the next few chapters, you will start to appreciate this claim as you start putting your ideas into action.

Meanwhile, let's delve into the remaining three aspects of achieving digital transformation.

Transform Products and services

A classic example to explain how and why products and services need digital transformation is the case of Netflix, the online streaming giant that we all are familiar with today. In 1997, Netflix was founded to sell and rent DVDs by mail, but changed to a subscription-based streaming service and also plays an active role in the production and distribution of its own content. While Netflix has become one of the largest entertainment companies that we all know of, many of its competitors, who started with the same business of renting out DVDs and VHS tapes, have now become extinct.

With the advent of broadband, Netflix was able to use the benefits of technology – advancements in internet streaming speed whereby consumers stopped measuring their internet speed in kbps (during the era of dial-up modems) and now measure their internet speeds in Mbps and even Gbps, with some ISPs using fiber optics. Netflix saw the opportunity to transform its business into a streaming service. There are several such examples where businesses have transformed their products or services by using advancements in technology.

The most important reason why other businesses and organizations have perished is due to their lack of willingness to transform their products and offerings. It is equally encouraging to see how some other organizations, and even certain classes of industries, have also come into being because of doing exactly the opposite. Digital technology is the foundation of their existence, and they never stop to evaluate and transform their services. The ride-sharing industry (such as Uber and Lyft) and home-sharing services (such as Airbnb and Vrbo) are all examples of this. A few more examples can be found in industries that are seeing this digital transition of their products and services, such as in-home fitness, gaming, and educational and professional development. There is a shift to provide products and services via a subscription model and delivered to your home either physically or virtually through the internet.

While these are some radical changes in industries that sell services, there have been some massive strides made by organizations selling products. With the advent of IoT devices, most of the products sold these days, ranging from home appliances such as a connected refrigerator or a smart TV, all the way to domestic and fighter aircraft, are all capable of generating enough telemetry to self-diagnose issues. This transforms the product from being an issue or defective into a product that can self-diagnose and heal these issues. This helps organizations build trust with their customers when it comes to the reliability and serviceability of these products. In the case of connected appliances, many appliance manufacturers get telemetry signals through IoT devices planted in them and can detect signals that tell them it's time to replace the air filter or water filter in a smart refrigerator and then offer value-added services such as sending replacement filters for a monthly subscription fee.

We have seen how products and services can be transformed by using the benefits of digital evolution to deliver a stellar customer experience and become a leader in the industry. We have also seen organizations carving out a net new niche industry.

Next, let's look at how digital transformation is applied to the backbone of any organization – its business operations, which power the organization to deliver its products and services to the customers on time, with the desired quality.

Streamline Operations

All sorts of processes and activities that take place within an organization that help it to deliver products or services are collectively referred to here as operations (sometimes referred to as business operations). Most organizations have well-defined processes or standard operating procedures to carry out day-to-day activities. As the maturity of the organization increases, so does the efficiency of these processes and procedures. However, while these models help to make the existing processes efficient, it is necessary to focus on partial or total transformation.

Going back to the example of 5G-connected cows, it might look and sound radical at the beginning, but it is becoming increasingly evident that hiring humans for mundane and repetitive tasks that don't need cognitive skills will become increasingly difficult due to what we discussed about the characteristics of the new evolving workforce. As technology keeps breaking barriers, it will make inroads into a lot of such legacy practices, processes, and procedures, even if they have managed to survive unchallenged for so many years.

One of the most elementary processes that happens in almost every organization dealing with products and services is the process of maintaining an inventory of raw materials or finished products or services being rendered on a day-to-day basis. There is a lot of manual effort involved here, and the process is often error-prone due to human involvement. To cite an example, a manufacturing firm that makes machines or cars will have a lot of components arriving as raw materials. If all the parts need to go through a quality assurance process and meet specifications and standards, it is not possible for humans to scale and ensure that all the raw materials meet the quality bar and even regulatory needs. This is where **artificial intelligence (AI)** and machine learning can be used to process large volumes of inspections. Cobots – collaborative robots – can also further augment human labor rather than replace it. By taking on dangerous, physically strenuous, and repetitive tasks, these new apps, bots, and automations are making factories safer and more efficient for employees.

To give a simpler relatable example, as a modern information worker, you must have seen organizations requiring employees to digitize documents such as receipts or manually type in massive amounts of data from invoices. This takes several hours of manual work, and it is often error-prone. However, in just a couple of hours, using the receipt processing capabilities of AI Builder, anybody can build an app that will automate this process and save several productive hours for the organization.

> **Important Note**
> If you want to learn more about AI Builder and prebuilt receipt processing, please see this link: `https://docs.microsoft.com/en-us/ai-builder/prebuilt-receipt-processing`.

Operations is a crucial function in any organization and, often, a new start-up or a developing organization struggles to streamline their operations, often neglecting the need for transformation of this vital backbone, often to their peril.

Now, let's look at the most important aspect, the foundation of any organization: happy customers! In the next section, let's see how digital transformation is shaping the future of customer experience and helping some organizations to embrace a customer-obsessed culture.

Exceed Customer expectations

There is a tremendous opportunity to influence customer expectations in the different phases of the customer life cycle, such as marketing, sales, acquisition, retaining, and servicing. While each of these processes represents an opportunity to use digital technology and improve the customer experience, given the purpose of this book, let's focus on a couple of aspects that will demonstrate the value of applying digital transformation to customer-related processes and thereby exceed customer expectations.

Organizations today are increasingly sensitive to their brand's reputation, especially on social media. Besides just targeting random folks for your marketing campaign, it is equally important to connect with each of these customers individually to build a long-term relationship. JetBlue Airways (jetBlue) is a major American airline that does a stellar job of providing a wonderful customer experience when dealing with complaints. On any given day, you will see this organization's Twitter handle trying to improve customer experience, whether related to a delay in takeoff, switching seats, or changing travel dates. Besides addressing customer issues, this Twitter-based help desk is also helping to build the brand's reputation as a customer-friendly organization, given the quick responses and near real-time resolution of customer issues. This is a very good representation of digital transformation applied to marketing, and it can also be categorized as the digital transformation of the customer service (servicing) life cycle too.

Let's take an example of an airline passenger who is stranded at an airport due to overbooking. The customer tries to reach the customer support department of the company through which the booking was done, and at least the first 5 to 10 minutes are lost in sharing basic details, such as the booking reference. Hopefully, after this, the customer service agent can resolve the case quickly and rebook this passenger. That would be an ideal situation, assuming you can get through to a customer service agent who understands what needs to be done. If you analyze this experience and how much time and money is being spent by the agent and the customer, then it becomes obvious that there is a great opportunity to improve this process. Therefore, many organizations have deployed some sort of automated voice assistant for phone calls, or chat bots on their sites, to deal with this. And with these digital assistants or bots, once you pass your booking reference number, it can pull all the information about the customer, provide all the information, and even re-book the customer using the customer's preferred date.

Besides providing huge savings for the booking/airline companies by cutting down the time spent by customer service agents on these calls, these digital assistants/bots also help to improve customer service expectations. Besides making drastic improvements to KPIs such as average response time, customer service cost, and first call resolution, this sort of automation helps bolster customer confidence in the organization and brand retention, which will be reflected in CSAT/NPS scores over the course of time.

Thus, the path of digital transformation rests on these four pillars, and you should now be in a position to appreciate what digital transformation is and why it is essential for the future existence of every organization, whether they are corporations, the public sector, health, the education sector, or anything else.

We are living in interesting times due to the COVID-19 pandemic, and it has helped us to learn and validate the benefits of digital transformation that some organizations were able to reap while others just perished. Businesses are connected and dependent on each other more than ever, customers are connected, and the velocity of change for their customers, their industry, and their supply chains is unprecedented. There is a level of agility that is required, and this can only be achieved by digital transformation.

> **Important Note**
> Many organizations, some your favorite brands, had to file
> bankruptcy and go out of business overnight. Here is a list of some
> of these organizations: `https://www.forbes.com/sites/`
> `hanktucker/2020/05/03/coronavirus-bankruptcy-`
> `tracker-these-major-companies-are-failing-amid-`
> `the-shutdown`.

It is abundantly clear that the digital transformation of the four pillars of your organization mentioned previously is imminent, and it has become more urgent than a "good to have" business objective, due to the changing economic conditions of current times.

Two of the most important factors that can contribute to the pace of this transformation are as follows:

- Availability of talent (skilled employees) to carry out this transformation
- Pace of transformation

This is where the role of low-code/no-code development platforms comes to the fore.

Introducing Microsoft Power Platform

Low-code/no-code development platforms are being provided by many technology companies, including Microsoft, Google, and Amazon, and they enable people who don't have professional development skills to be able to build solutions for the needs of their organization.

As mentioned in earlier sections of this chapter, there are two major benefits of these platforms:

- A shallow or almost non-existent learning curve for training new folks

- The speed (productivity) at which these solutions can be built and deployed

One such promising platform is Microsoft Power Platform. Power Platform is a low-code/no-code platform that consists of a suite of products that enable organizations to not just accelerate digital transformation but also spread the viral adoption of these skills across the organization. It is a suite of low-code/no-code products, as shown in the following diagram:

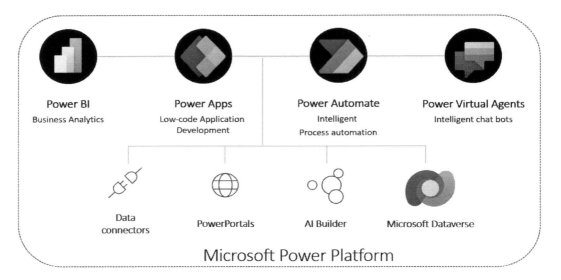

Figure 1.3 – Microsoft Power Platform Components

Here are the important constituents of Microsoft Power Platform:

- **Power BI**: Empowers you to visualize and discover insights hidden in your data with Microsoft Power BI.

- **Power Apps**: Enables everyone to build and share business apps quickly, using no or very little code.

- **Power Automate**: Helps you to configure automated workflows that can be triggered on demand or scheduled to execute at set intervals to take care of business needs or enforce business logic.

- **Power Virtual Agents**: Provides everyone with a platform to easily build intelligent chatbots without any coding.

- **Microsoft Dataverse**: Easily structures a variety of data and business logic to support interconnected applications and processes in a secure and compliant manner.

- **AI Builder**: Democratizes the use of **Artificial Intelligence (AI)** to enhance your apps and business process, without having to write any code. Just bring your data, train the model, which is generated by the platform, and start integrating it into your applications. AI Builder is available as a feature within Power Apps that enables you to add intelligence such as object recognition, prediction, and form processing into your apps.

- **Data connectors**: You can easily integrate with various data sources within the organization through 350+ built-in data connectors.

- **Portals**: Power Apps portals enable you to interact with your customers, who are external to your organization, as well as enable internal employees to interact with business data stored in Microsoft Dataverse.

Given the entire suite of products included in the Power Platform, a citizen developer has enough tools at their disposal to carry out a world of transformations.

So, who is a citizen developer, and why are you, or may you soon become, a citizen developer?

Becoming a citizen developer

Citizen developer refers to any set of employees who may not have been hired to write code or work on traditional development tasks as their daily job, but with low-code/no-code platforms and limited professional support from traditional developers, these employees can build solutions for their organization, its customers, or to boost their own efficiency.

The term was originally coined by analysts at Gartner and is now widely adopted to refer to anyone who uses these low-code/no-code platforms.

As an organization, there is no more worrying about a dearth of skilled employees to kickstart an organization's digital transformation and, in fact, you will be converting and adding more resources to the pool every day.

As a citizen developer, you will enjoy the new-found freedom of being able to create a new solution without a steep learning curve, and trust us: once you are hooked, it is pretty addictive!

Besides this, once you have acquired skills as a citizen developer, you will have the confidence to sign up for bigger and bolder challenges as part of the digital transformation journey in your organization.

Now that you are aware of citizen developers and Microsoft Power Platform, it is time to introduce Microsoft Dataverse for Teams.

Microsoft Dataverse for Teams

Microsoft Power Platform is now getting integrated with Microsoft Teams to enable organizations to tailor Microsoft 365 to their needs and empower citizen developers to make greater use of the collaboration capabilities of Teams. Microsoft Dataverse for Teams blends with a set of Power Platform products and features that are integrated into the Microsoft Teams experience and provides data storage with different data types, security, and governance, as well as one-click solution deployments. These solution deployments enable easy portability of custom-built solutions across different teams and environments, or acquired solutions that are built by third-party ISVs and published in Microsoft AppSource.

In the next chapter, we will see how Microsoft Dataverse for Teams enables citizen developers to easily build and deploy apps and intelligent chatbots in Teams with Power Apps, Power Automate Flows, and Power Virtual Agents. Additionally, citizen developers can now easily create custom data tables to store business data that can be used by these apps, chatbots, and flows, besides ensuring robust security and governance features that allow you to control access to these apps, bots, and flows, as well as their underlying data. All of this can be achieved without leaving the Teams application!

Microsoft Dataverse for Teams, along with the Power Platform in Teams, makes app building and the automation of tasks so simple that most of the employees in any organization can pick up the skills required in a matter of hours. This claim will be validated soon, when you get to the next chapter of this book!

Summary

To summarize, in this chapter we have seen how digital evolution has shaped our personal lives, as well as organizations. We have also seen what digital transformation is and why it is a must for every organization to be ready for ongoing transformation.

We learned about low-code/no-code platforms and how platforms such as Microsoft Power Platform and Microsoft Dataverse for Teams can help you to accelerate digital transformation in your organization. This fundamental knowledge is essential to appreciate and build competency as a citizen developer. You could be part of the team implementing this digital transformation as a digital transformation agent or a leader initiating and championing the cause of digital transformation within your organization.

Finally, the last and most important aspect is the contribution of citizen developers to this digital transformation endeavor, while also gaining significant skills to help their own careers.

In the next chapter, *Exploring Microsoft Dataverse for Teams*, we will dig deeper into the different Power Platform components and Microsoft Dataverse, and explore how you can use the different components while building an app or a full-fledged end-to-end business solution.

2

Exploring Microsoft Dataverse for Teams

In the previous chapter, we were introduced to **Microsoft Dataverse for Teams**, which helps you to build apps, bots, and flows with minimum training. In this chapter, we will try to learn more about Microsoft Dataverse for Teams and the various components of **Power Platform** that form the foundation of this low-code/no-code platform experience within Microsoft Teams.

Since data is at the heart of any business application that you build, it is important to understand the data platform involved here. In this chapter, we will learn about the various components of Power Platform and Microsoft Dataverse for Teams.

In this chapter, we will explore the following topics:

- Exploring Microsoft Dataverse for Teams
- Exploring Power Apps
- Exploring Power Automate
- Exploring Power Virtual Agents
- Understanding Data Connectors

There is a lightweight version of the Power Platform suite included inside the Microsoft Teams experience, comprising **Power Apps**, **Power Automate**, **Power Virtual Agents**, **Data Connectors**, and a lightweight version of Microsoft Dataverse, known as Microsoft Dataverse for Teams.

The following diagram should help you get a good idea of the composition of the Power Platform suite:

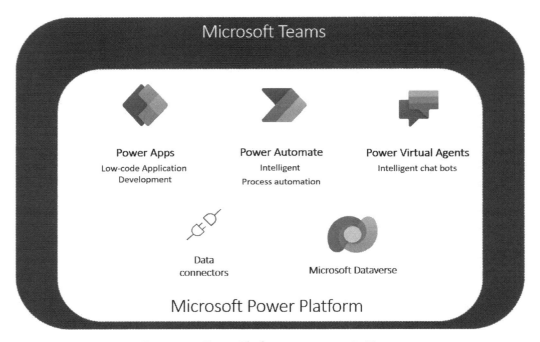

Figure 2.1 – Power Platform components in Teams

As we continue exploring each of these components, you will appreciate these components and their value to the **citizen development** experience.

Exploring Microsoft Dataverse for Teams

Microsoft Dataverse is a data platform that allows you to store and model a variety of data and business logic to support interconnected applications and processes in a secure and compliant manner.

Microsoft Dataverse for Teams is a lightweight data platform that allows you to store and model a variety of data for Microsoft Teams, such that Power Apps applications, Power Automate flows, and Power Virtual Agent bots built within Microsoft Teams can leverage most of these data platform features.

Dataverse for Teams allows you to create tables with columns of different data types, such as **Text**, **Number**, **Phone**, and **Email**, as seen in the following screenshot:

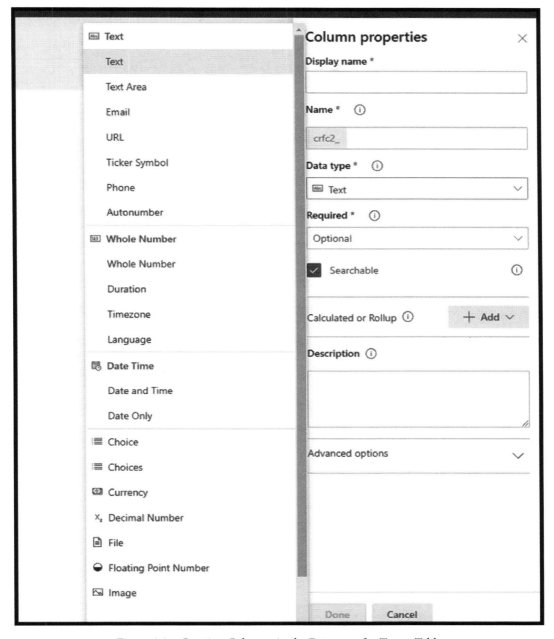

Figure 2.2 – Creating Columns in the Dataverse for Teams Table

Some of the salient features of Microsoft Dataverse for Teams are as follows:

- Microsoft Dataverse for Teams allows citizen developers to use relational storage, such as tables, for defining structured schema and relationships, along with support for data types such as number, text, and options (also known as choices).

- Team owners can control the security of the data using built-in roles as per the **OMGA (Owners, Members, Guests**, and **App Users)** model. *Owners* refers to the owner of the team, *Members* refers to the team members, *App Users* refers to the group of people outside the team, but within your organization, who require access, and *Guests* are people outside your organization who a team owner invites for collaboration, such as a partner organization or consultants.

- Microsoft Dataverse for Teams also allows citizen developers to search and install pre-built industry solutions or solutions within your organization from a gallery, in the same way as you would install apps for your mobile device from a standard app store.

In the following screenshot, you can see that an app maker can create columns as per the needs of the application by choosing **First Name**, **Text** for the **Last Name** field, **Phone** for the **Contact No** field, and **Email** as the **Email** data type:

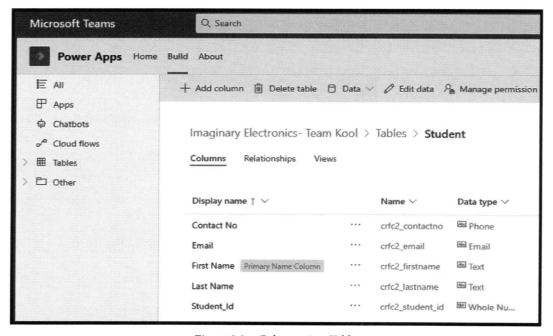

Figure 2.3 – Columns in a Table

This ensures that the data entered in these columns is validated by the platform to ensure that a valid email address format was provided by the user, for example.

We will see the detailed step-by-step instructions on how to create a table and columns with Dataverse for Teams when we start building our first application in *Chapter 3, Building Your First App with Microsoft Dataverse for Teams*.

Once the table and column definitions are ready, you will be able to use the Edit data button and add data to a new screen, as shown in the following screenshot:

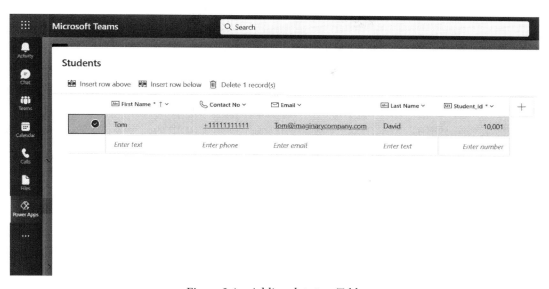

Figure 2.4 – Adding data to a Table

In the preceding *screenshot*, you can see that the data gets linked to appropriate handling protocols that allow you to use default applications to handle the data. For example, if you click on the phone number, it will automatically try to dial the number using the default calling application installed, which will be Microsoft Teams in this case. Similarly, with email, it will open a new draft email with your default mail client application such as Office Outlook, Windows Mail, or any other app that is the default on your machine. All this automatic handling of data and default actions is determined by Dataverse for Teams based on the data type that was chosen for the column. In the same **Edit data** screen as in the preceding screenshot, you have the option to keep adding more columns while adding data simultaneously.

This same data can also be edited using the Microsoft Excel client, as shown in the following screenshot:

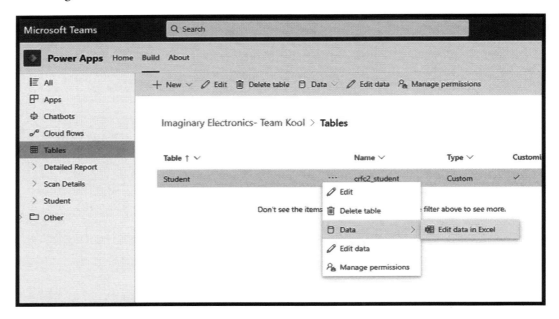

Figure 2.5 – Editing Table data in Excel

> **Editing data**
>
> Please refer to this blog for details on how the data in a table can be edited using Excel: `https://powerapps.microsoft.com/en-us/blog/use-edit-in-excel-in-dataverse-for-teams/`.

Dataverse for Teams tables are logically part of the same environment where you will see **Apps, Chatbots**, and **Flows**. An **Environment** is like a virtual container for all parts of Power Platform that are logically related or dependent on the same set of data or just co-located for business reasons. Today, with Dataverse for Teams, there is a one-to-one mapping of each Dataverse for Teams environment with a Microsoft **Team**.

A Dataverse for Teams environment should work for your regular application in a team; however, as the applications grow and mature, there will be a need to make this application available to a larger audience outside of your team, or the data collected will continue to grow beyond the capacity limits supported by Dataverse for Teams. In such cases, Dataverse for Teams can be upgraded to a Dataverse environment – in other words, when you need additional control, capabilities, or capacity, you have the option to upgrade.

Capacity limits with Dataverse for Teams

Current capacity limits with Dataverse for Teams are documented at the following link: `https://docs.microsoft.com/en-us/power-platform/admin/about-teams-environment#capacity-limits`.

You can view all the environments in the Power Platform admin center (`https://admin.powerplatform.microsoft.com/environments`). Please ensure that you are signed in to your organization account before accessing this link. Once you are in the admin center, you will be able to see all the environments for which you are designated as the system administrator, including the ones that you created:

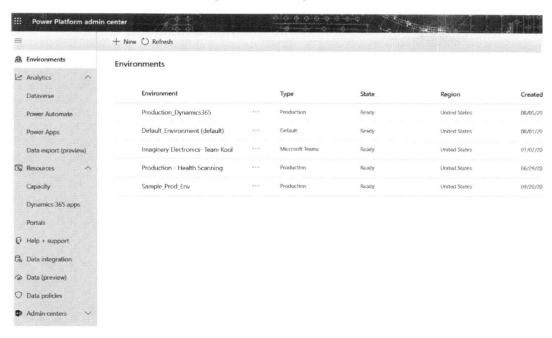

Figure 2.6 – Different types of environments in the Power Platform Admin Center

As seen in the preceding screenshot, you will see different types of environments (**Microsoft Teams**, **Default**, and **Production**). The **Microsoft Teams** type is the one such environment that contains the data from the corresponding Teams that you create. You will see one Teams type for each environment corresponding to Microsoft Teams where you created tables, Power Apps applications, Power Automate flows, or Power Virtual Agent bots.

Default and **Production** are types of Dataverse environments that we will learn about in *Chapter 8, Managing the Application Life Cycle and Environment Life Cycle.*

We'll dive deeper into the features of Microsoft Dataverse in *Chapter 5, Understanding Microsoft Dataverse.*

In this section, you got a good introduction to what Microsoft Dataverse for Teams is along with its capabilities. In the next section, we will continue to look at other Power Platform components that are now part of Microsoft Teams.

Exploring Power Apps

Power Apps is the user experience platform that allows everyone to build low-code/no-code applications quickly and with very little experience. With Power Apps, you have containers that handle layouts and the flow of controls on the screen while running the application on different devices with different form factors. Power Apps provides you with an app-building experience in the maker experience portal, which can be found at `https://make.powerapps.com`.

With Microsoft Dataverse for Teams, this maker experience (a studio or visual editor where you make or create new apps) is now embedded within the Microsoft Teams application. The benefit of Microsoft Dataverse for Teams is that you don't need additional licenses, outside of the Teams or Office 365 licenses, to run these applications. To use these applications as standalone applications outside of Teams, in a browser, for example, users are expected to have additional Power Apps licenses.

Here is what the experience looks like when this maker portal is made available within the Microsoft Teams application:

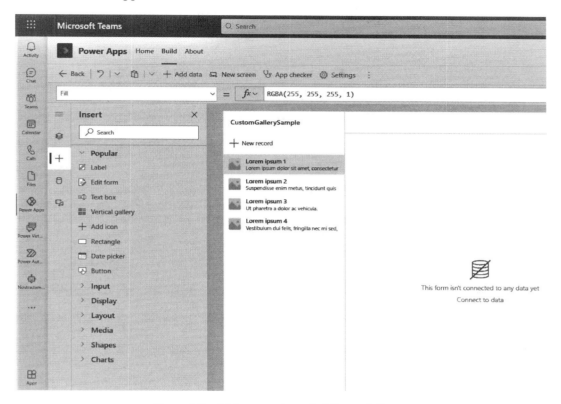

Figure 2.7 – Maker experience in Microsoft Teams

We will learn more about how to get to this screen and start building apps in *Chapter 3, Building Your First App with Microsoft Dataverse for Teams*.

Let's now take a quick look at Power Automate and understand how Power Automate can be helpful in automating a lot of tasks for citizen developers.

Exploring Power Automate

Power Automate provides the automation platform that helps you to automate time-consuming, repetitive tasks. A good scenario, from the student enrolment example cited earlier, would be that of automating sending an email summary of the classes that the student signed up for. Such repetitive, mundane tasks can be quickly automated using a flow, without using a single line of code. Power Automate provides a simple flow designer on `https://flow.microsoft.com/`. This is where you can create standalone flows; however, with Dataverse for Teams, there are multiple places where you can create your flows, with one such scenario illustrated in the following screenshot:

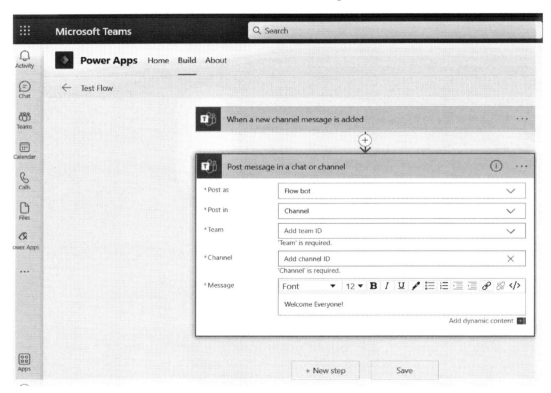

Figure 2.8 – Power Automate Experience in Microsoft Teams

Using simple steps, any citizen developer can stitch together an automated flow with just a few clicks. You can schedule a recurring task, which will retrieve messages from a Microsoft Teams channel, and can then send an SMS using the Twilio connector.

Once such flows are created, you can run them from within Teams depending on a trigger, either on a set schedule or some standard triggers as configured. A trigger is the occurrence of an event for which certain predefined actions are executed. In this case, the triggers can be a button pressed within your application or data being inserted or a change of state in the data, for example, when the state of an application changes to approved or rejected. In the preceding screenshot, you can see that the trigger for the flow to be invoked is whenever a message is posted to the Teams channel.

We will dive deeper into Power Automate within Teams in *Chapter 5, Understanding Microsoft Dataverse*.

Let's now look at another interesting component of Power Platform that is very useful in providing customer service experiences through chatbots – Power Virtual Agents.

Exploring Power Virtual Agents

Power Virtual Agents (**PVAs**) are used to build intelligent chatbots, rapidly and without the need to write any code. It provides you with a fast and intuitive way to build bots that help customers of these bots to make decisions or take certain actions. The bot will not just be a conversational bot, but will also offer a set of interactions and experiences that appear natural, as if you were talking to a human customer service agent. It leverages natural language understanding to parse the questions asked by the customer and can match them syntactically or semantically to provide the best response to the customer.

As regards a bot, you begin with a topic that can be authored by typing in questions before moving to the bot authoring experience, which you can see in the following screenshot:

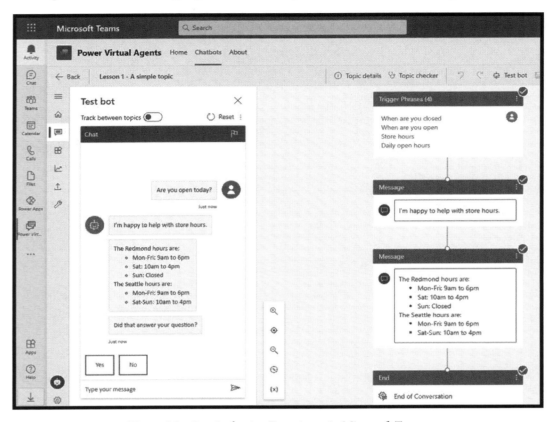

Figure 2.9 – Bot Authoring Experience in Microsoft Teams

You get a fully integrated bot authoring experience, which helps you to check the topics and validate and test the bot experience as you build it, side by side, as seen in the preceding screenshot, and this experience of bot creation is now available in Microsoft Teams.

Once the bot is authored in a particular team, the author (citizen developer) can publish this and then share it with the intended audience. Sharing a published bot with users entails a couple of options based on the flow:

- Share it with the team where it is created.
- Submit it for approval to the Teams administrator, so that the bot can be made available to everyone within your organization.

Submitting this to the Teams administrator for approval helps the administrator to be in control and maintain the enterprise governance aspect. The administrator gets to approve or reject these bots from being made available to all teams within the organization.

We have seen how these Power Virtual Agent bots empower citizen developers with yet another wonderful tool to usher in a wave of digital transformation, especially in areas that require front desk or customer service life cycle issues to be handled, support tickets to be issued, or problems to be managed.

Let's now look at another important component of the Power Platform experience within Teams: Data Connectors.

Understanding Data Connectors

Data Connectors are the magic glue that helps you to bind your application, bot, or flow with any data store, including Microsoft Dataverse. These connectors allow citizen developers to connect to hundreds of standard business data stores, such as Adobe, Amazon Redshift, Azure Blob Storage, Azure Data Explorer, Dropbox, IBM DB2, DocuSign, Dynamics NAV, and Salesforce, in addition to social platforms such as Twitter, Facebook, and Instagram. Professional developers can extend this model to build custom connectors to any data platform with public API support. As seen in the following screenshot, you can easily bring in the data from any of these data platforms listed earlier and quickly create low code/no-code applications to interact with this set of data:

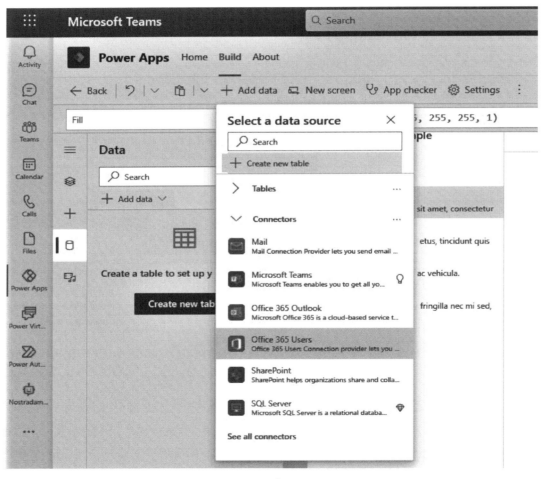

Figure 2.10 – List of Data Connectors

With Data Connectors, the citizen developer doesn't need to know the details about the underlying connection mechanisms implemented. All the technology and configuration details are abstracted away, making it easier to connect with a multitude of data sources. There are more than 300 data connectors available, with more being added at regular intervals. Connectors are broadly classified into **Standard**, **Premium**, and **Custom**. Standard connectors can be used by anyone with Office licenses, and so are available in Dataverse for Teams at no additional cost. Premium connectors require users of the flow to have a Power Automate or Power Apps license. Custom connectors, as the name indicates, are used to connect external web services for which there are no standard or premium connectors available. These web services could be specific to your application or organization. If you wish to get your custom connector publicly available to all users of the product, you can get it certified by Microsoft by using the documentation available at this link: `https://docs.microsoft.com/en-us/connectors/custom-connectors/submit-certification`.

For a complete list of connections, please refer to the following link: `https://docs.microsoft.com/en-us/connectors/connector-reference/connector-reference-powerapps-connectors#list-of-connectors`.

Summary

Throughout this chapter, you have developed a good understanding of Microsoft Dataverse for Teams. You have also looked at each of these components – Power Apps, Power Automate, Power Virtual Agents, and Microsoft Dataverse for Teams – and how they come together to empower citizen developers to build low-code/no-code applications, flows, and bots, and thereby usher in the era of digital transformation within their organizations.

In the next chapter, we will look at building our first application using Microsoft Dataverse for Teams. This application will be a health scan application, very relevant in current times, which can be leveraged by most organizations that require a physical presence on site, be it in offices, construction sites, hospitals, or schools.

3
Building Your First App with Microsoft Dataverse for Teams

In the previous chapter, we learned about Microsoft **Dataverse for Teams** and the various components of **Power Platform** that form the foundation of the low-code/no-code platform experience within Microsoft Teams. In this chapter, we are going to build our first application using Microsoft Dataverse for Teams.

In this chapter, we will build our first application, **Health Scanner**, using Microsoft Dataverse. This application can be used to keep a record of health statistics of employees or students prior to starting a shift or when present in a classroom.

The important topics that will be covered are as follows:

- Getting Started
- Data Modeling for Applications
- Introducing the Power Apps Build Hub in Teams
- Creating a Dataverse table
- Building your first app

Let's look at the first topic – *Getting Started*, which will help you to understand the prerequisites on licensing, which will allow you to sign in to the application.

Getting Started

To build an application using Power Apps and Microsoft Dataverse for Teams, all you need is an applicable Microsoft 365 license (earlier known as Office 365). There are several offers to choose from, and you can compare all the different plans for businesses and enterprises using this link: `https://www.microsoft.com/en-us/microsoft-365/business/compare-all-microsoft-365-business-products`.

Microsoft Power Platform doesn't require you to have a license for building (making) applications, and license checks are made only when the apps are consumed (during runtime). This means that the end users of your application need to be appropriately licensed to be able to run applications built on Power Platform.

Using the link mentioned, you or your tenant administrator should be able to procure the Microsoft 365 license and assign it to you. To assign a license, you need to be a **Global Administrator**, **License Administrator**, or **User Administrator**. In an organization, depending on the size and roles, each of these roles could be played by a different individual. Once you have a role that allows you to assign a license, navigate to **Microsoft 365 admin center** | **Users** | **Active Users** and then assign a Microsoft 365 license, as shown in the following screenshot:

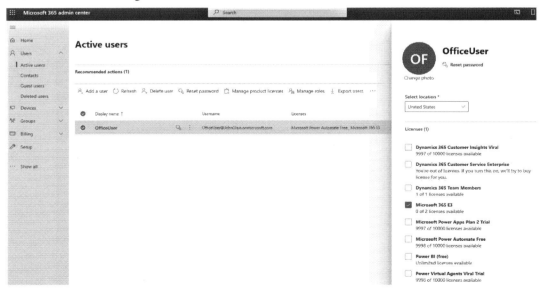

Figure 3.1 – Assigning a license in the Microsoft 365 admin center

> **More information**
>
> For more instructions on how a license can be assigned to users using the Microsoft 365 admin center, please refer to the instructions here: `https://docs.microsoft.com/en-us/microsoft-365/admin/manage/assign-licenses-to-users?view=o365-worldwide`.

We will be taking a deeper look at some more licensing aspects in *Chapter 11*, *Licensing for Microsoft Dataverse and Dataverse for Teams*.

Once a Microsoft 365 license is assigned, you are all set to sign in and get started with building your first application. To illustrate this, let's say your name is **OfficeUser** and this user will sign in using a username/email as *OfficeUser@<yourdomain>.onmicrosoft.com*, where your domain represents the name of the tenant's domain.

Once you log in, launch a browser and type in `https://teams.microsoft.com/`. You could also use the desktop client (Microsoft Teams application) and log in. If you are already logged in, you will land on the home page, which should look like the following screenshot:

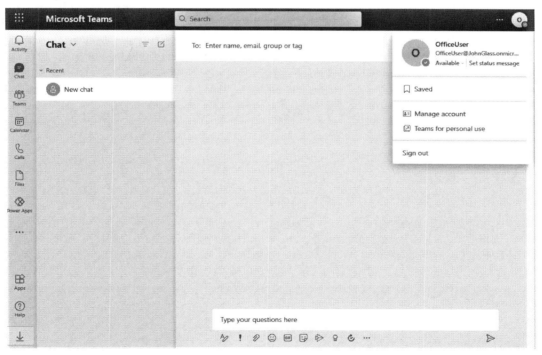

Figure 3.2 – Successful login into Microsoft Teams

Once you are logged in, you are all set to start creating your application. In the next section, we will do data modeling for the **Health Scanner** application.

Data Modeling for Applications

As mentioned earlier in this chapter, for the first application, we will build a **Health Scanner** application. This app will be a general-purpose application that can be used by any organization to scan the health of their employees, customers, or any other visitors. In the case of this chapter, this application will be built as a simple application that will capture the basic health diagnostic data before and after a working shift.

To do this, let's start thinking of the basic set of information that our Health Scanner application needs to capture and store. This information set includes the following data:

- **Employee ID**
- **First Name** and **Last Name**
- **Phone Number**
- **Email**
- **Scan Date**
- **Body Temperature**
- **Questions**, such as "Have you experienced a cough or shortness of breath – Yes/No?"
- **A self-declaration**, such as "I acknowledge that the information I've given is accurate and complete – Yes/No?"

This is just a representative data model to be used for illustration purposes in this chapter, and you may extend the schema to include more information/data depending on regulatory needs, and as required by the local health authority and organization policies.

For a simple application, this data could go into a single table, or you could make two or more tables, if you wish to maintain the employee information, such as **ID**, **Name**, **Phone Number**, and **Email address**, in a separate table, or leverage the out-of-box table in Dataverse known as **User**. While this approach of two different tables – one for employee master information and one for diagnostic data – might work for our example here, it may not be required for some other scenarios, such as visitor scanning, as the information about visitors might not be something that needs to be persisted in a separate table as master data. A separate table for employees makes sense as this is typically what the HR department of any organization would like to have or would already have in their systems.

To begin with, let's start with a single table containing all this information. In the next section, we will see how to get started with the Power Apps **Build** Hub, where a Dataverse table can be created based on the data model we built here.

Introducing the Power Apps Build Hub in Teams

To create a Dataverse table, we need to get started by adding **Power Apps** to the Team. To do this, follow these instructions:

1. Click the **More added apps** button (the three dots on the left side of the screen), as shown in the following screenshot:

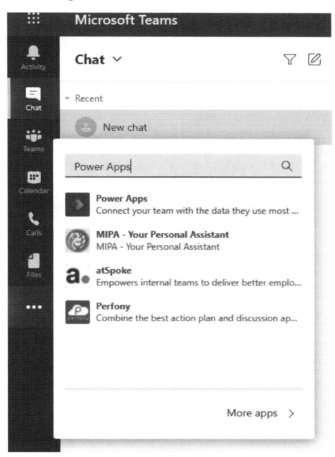

Figure 3.3 – Searching for Power Apps in Microsoft Teams

2. Type in Power Apps and choose it from the options that appear. A page about Power Apps will pop up:

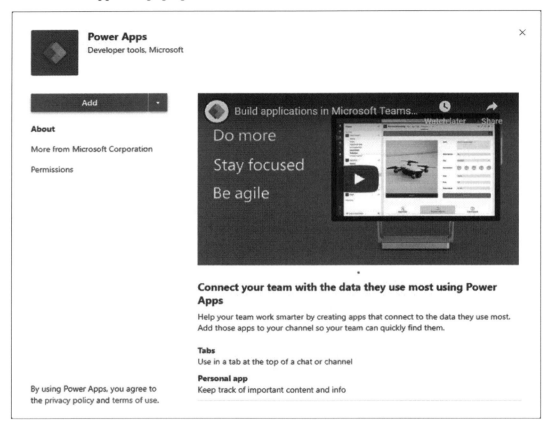

Figure 3.4 – Adding Power Apps to Microsoft Teams

3. Click the **Add** option, and you will have successfully added Power Apps to Microsoft Teams. Power Apps can also be added by using the Apps flyout menu in the lower-left corner, which opens the Apps store in Microsoft Teams:

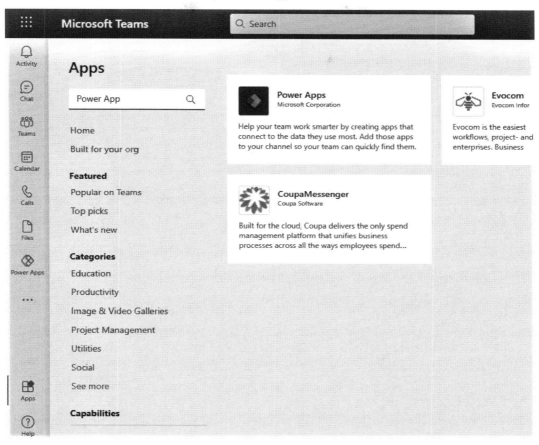

Figure 3.5 – Adding Power Apps from the Apps store in Teams

4. To avoid repeating these steps of adding Power Apps every time, you must pin the Power Apps app to Teams by right-clicking and then selecting the **Pin** option, as seen in the following screenshot:

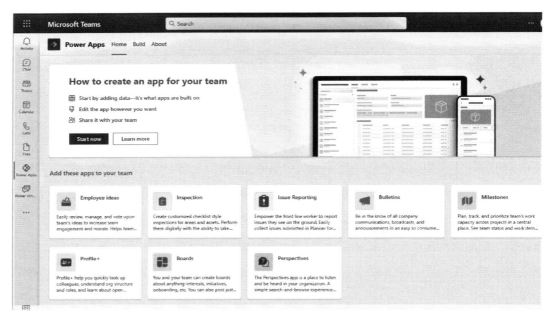

Figure 3.6 – Pinning Power Apps to the Teams navigation panel

This ensures that the Power Apps option is always displayed, as a shortcut, on the Teams left navigation panel, even after you navigate away from this screen.

5. Once you have added and pinned Power Apps to Teams, as seen in the previous snapshot, you will land on the **Home** screen. On the **Home** screen itself, you can click **Start now** directly or navigate to the **Build** tab and then get started with creating an app. Once you click this option, you will be prompted with this new pop-up screen, as shown in the following screenshot:

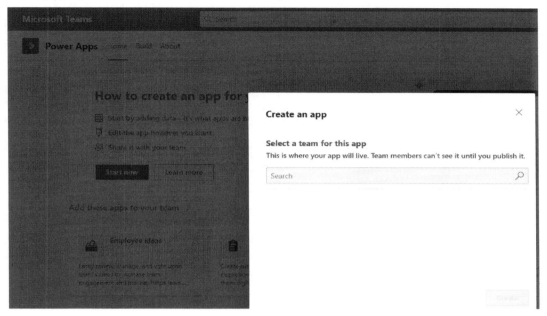

Figure 3.7 – Selecting a team for the app

Since you haven't created any teams or joined any teams, no teams are shown in the options list.

6.   At this point, let's move on to creating a team that can be used as a home for this app. For this, you will have to navigate to the Teams icon on the left-hand navigation panel:

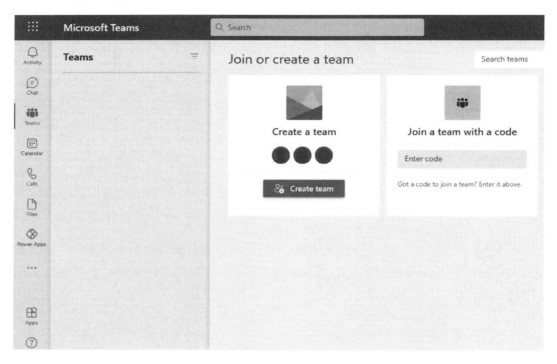

Figure 3.8 – Creating a team for your app

7. Quite often, if your organization uses Microsoft Teams, it is likely that you are already part of some team or you are aware of a team that you could join, either by using a code generated by the Team owner or by searching by team and then requesting to join, as seen in the following screenshot:

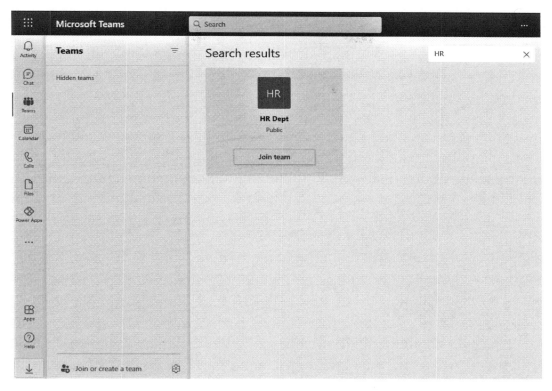

Figure 3.9 – Joining a team

8. For the sake of this example, let's create a new team for our app here from scratch. Once you click **Create**, there is an option to create a team **From scratch** or **From a group or team** that already exists in Microsoft 365:

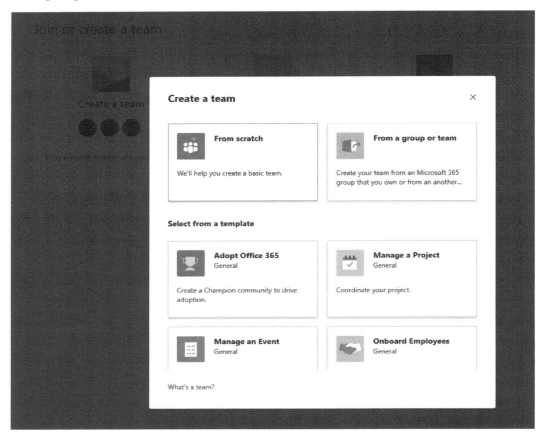

Figure 3.10 – Creating a team from scratch

Important Note

More information on Microsoft 365 groups can be found at `https://docs.microsoft.com/en-us/microsoft-365/admin/create-groups/office-365-groups?view=o365-worldwide`.

---

9. Clicking through the wizard, let's create this team by using some random name; we'll go for `Imaginary Electronics- Team Kool`, as seen in the following screenshot. For now, you will be the only member on this team, but you are free to add more people within the organization to this team. These new members who will be added to this team will be consumers or users of your application.

10. Let's now add a few more users within your organization who will be the intended users of the Health Scanner application. If you are the owner of any team, you can always add **members** at any point using the **Add member** option, as shown in the following screenshot:

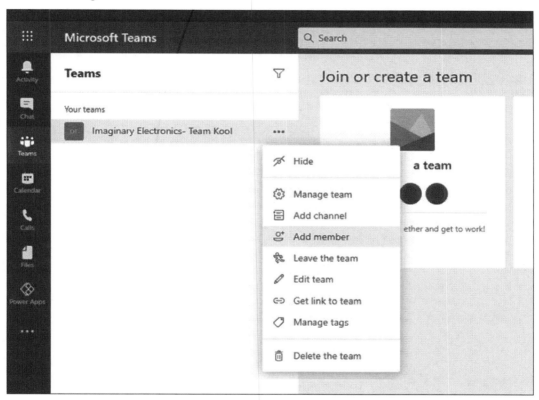

Figure 3.11 – Adding member(s) to a team

These newly added members can perform modifications in terms of customizing/ extending the applications within Dataverse for Teams.

11. Now that the team has been created, let's continue with creating the app in this newly created team – **Imaginary Electronics- Team Kool**. For this, we will have to go back to the Power Apps Build Hub and resume app creation. This time, the dropdown for **Select a team** is now populated with the name of our new team:

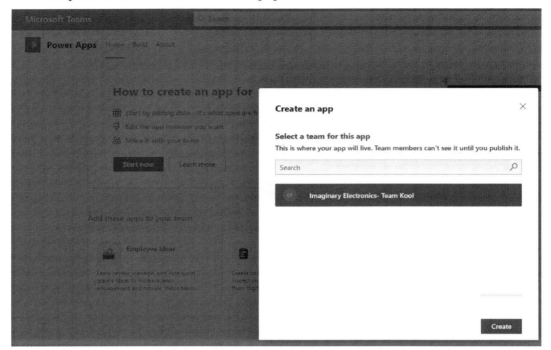

Figure 3.12 – Team available for the app

12. Once the team is selected, you will see Power Apps automatically setting up the team and application, until it prompts you to provide the name of the new app to be created. Here, you can enter the name Health Scanner and hit the **Save** button.

This sets up the stage for you to start creating a table in Dataverse, which we will see in the next section.

Creating a Dataverse table

In this section, we will be creating a new table that will help you to store the application data that the users of your app will be entering or viewing. Let's look at how a new table is created:

1. As seen in the following screenshot, once the new app name is provided, the screen will have options shown for **Create new table**:

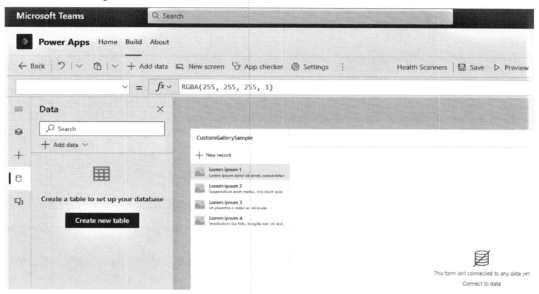

Figure 3.13 – The Create new table option

2. Once you click the **Create new table** button, you will be prompted to provide a table name. Let's name the table Scan Details.

3. This will take us to the table definition screen where the columns, as determined in our data modeling exercise earlier, can be created. On this screen, as illustrated in the following screenshot, you will see a column that is auto created, with the column name of **Name**:

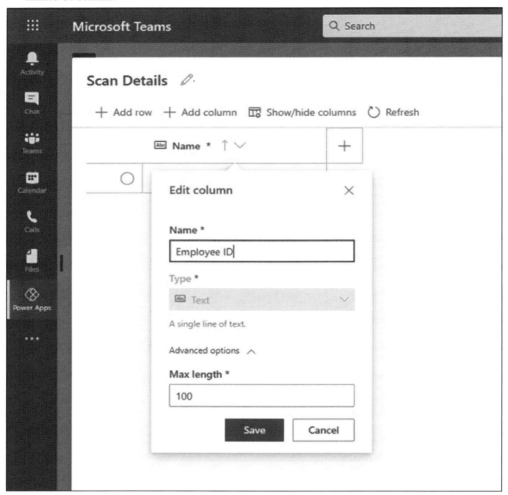

Figure 3.14 – Defining the first column

This **Name** column represents a unique name or identifier for each record created inside the table. As in our example, this would be an Employee ID to uniquely identify an employee.

4. Let's edit this column to be renamed as Employee ID, using the down arrow/ chevron control next to the text of the column name, **Name**, as shown in the preceding screenshot.

5. Next, using the + control, you can add other columns required by the data model. In the preceding screenshot, you will see that during the creation of these columns, you have the option to select the right data type (**Text, Email, URL, Phone, Auto number, Number, Date, Decimal, Lookup, Choice, Yes/No**) option, depending on the type of data expected in these columns:

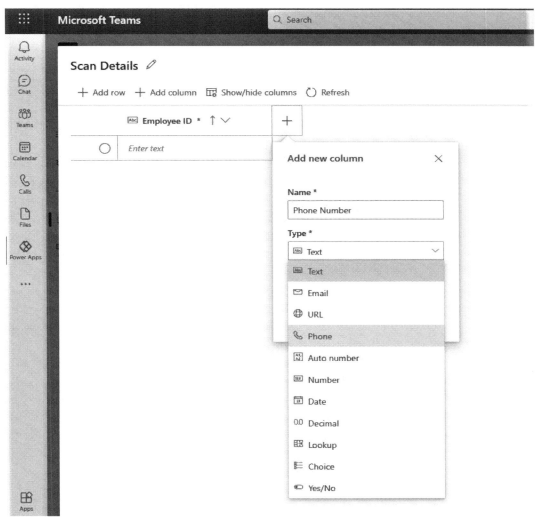

Figure 3.15 – Different data types to suit the needs of your data model

6. Once all the columns are created as per their data type, as seen in the following screenshot, there is an option to additionally provide data as well, along with the definition. For this, you need to keep adding rows using the **Add row** control on the same screen:

Figure 3.16 – Adding columns and rows to the table

7. Hitting the **Close** button at the bottom of the screen commits the data to the Dataverse, and the schema is then updated with this new table. The default screen for **Health Scanner** is presented as seen in the following screenshot:

Figure 3.17 – Default landing screen for the app

You have just built your first table in Microsoft Dataverse and you may notice that it is already starting to take the shape of an application. You may need to fix the **Data source** property of the **BrowseGallery1** control, setting it to the **Scan Details** table, to start seeing the data.

In the next section, we will learn about creating new screen elements and screens to build your first app.

Building your first app

As you saw in the previous section, as soon as the table was created, the app screen was ready for you to get started with building your application. In this section, you will continue to add the remaining items to your app and rearrange a few screen elements to get the app ready to publish. Before that, let's explore a few interesting things about the app that was autogenerated for you.

Exploring the app elements

In this section, we will browse through the autogenerated app and study a few elements of the app before deciding to customize it to suit our needs:

1. Hit the **Preview** button in the top-right corner of the app, as seen in the preceding screenshot. That will launch the skeletal app or the initial version in preview mode, for you to run, test, and debug. You can start entering some scan data for employees (such as **Employee ID**, **First Name**, **Phone Number**, and **Body Temperature**), as shown in the following screenshot:

Figure 3.18 – Entering data from the app

The arrangement of the fields on this screen may not be in the order that you would expect for collecting this information. In fact, you never arranged them in the first place; this was the default placement implemented by Power Apps.

2. After entering and saving your data, exit out of the Preview experience and try rearranging the form elements (also known as fields on the screen), as shown in the following screenshot:

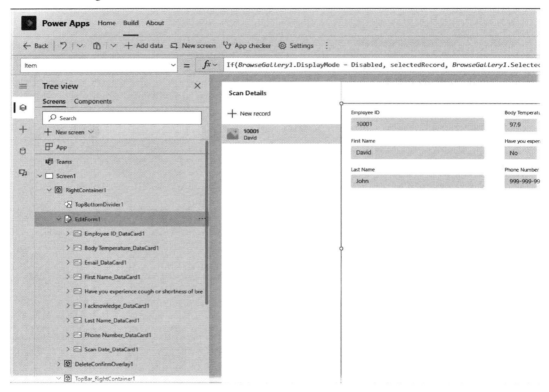

Figure 3.19 – Screens of the app

3. In the preceding screenshot, as you can see, the screen components are arranged in a hierarchy. Let's take a quick look at them to understand what they are and how we can play with them to customize our application much better. At the top of the hierarchy is **Screen**, and then you have **RightContainer1** and **LeftContainer1**, separated by **LeftRightDivider1**. Expanding the top-right element – **RightContainer1** – will reveal more elements, including dividers, containers, and forms (represented as **EditForm1**), shown in the following screenshot:

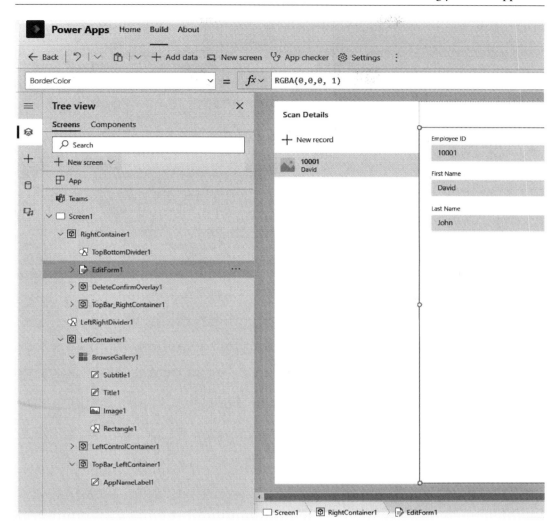

Figure 3.20 – Screen elements of the app

You can observe that these screen elements, such as **RightContainer1** and **LeftRightDivider1**, have numbers as a suffix in their name or identifiers; these are autogenerated by the platform to uniquely identify them. You can rename these screen elements and they can be customized by changing their properties as per your needs. Some organizations have coding conventions (rules), such as all buttons need to have the prefix **btn**, or form names should start with **frm_**.

RightContainer1 represents a **Container** element that holds a logical set of controls and has its own set of properties. A **Container** helps to automatically reflow and resize controls within them to enable easy and responsive layouts. They help your app to scale the screen in devices with different form factors, without any additional work required from your end. As seen in the preceding screenshot, when you click each of these screen elements, there is a panel on the right of the screen that displays the element details and properties, such as position, size, and border color. Similarly, if you expand the **EditForm1** field, you will see all the columns that you created in the data model have been placed on this form, as a **Card**. A card works as a container of the **Field name** – **Field value** pair and is mapped to a column in the table through the **DataField** property. As seen in the following screenshot, each of the column values (for example, **First Name**) is represented as a card – such as **First Name_DataCard1**, which is mapped to **DataField crfc2_firstname**:

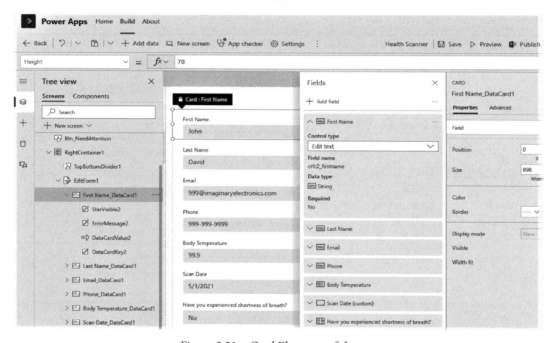

Figure 3.21 – Card Elements of the app

In the preceding screenshot, the card, **First Name_DataCard1**, is holding the label (**First Name**) and the value **John**.

Here, **crfc2_firstname** is the name of your column in the table schema, which is a unique name across this team environment. The prefix **crfc2_** is a system-generated prefix to ensure uniqueness (as you can imagine, **firstname** can be a column name in any table that will be created, in future, within any such team environment. Now, by modifying the **Position** and **Size** values of various cards on the right container, you can rearrange the fields on the screen. Additionally, you can now change the text of the field to be more descriptive, as seen in the following screenshot:

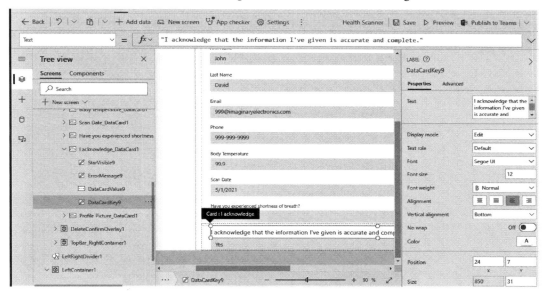

Figure 3.22 – Text property of the card

4. Next, in the **Card: I acknowledge** field, the value of the text field is changed from **Parent.DisplayName** to the text value I acknowledge that the information I've given is accurate and complete..

> **Unlocking controls**
>
> Occasionally, you may find some elements or controls to be locked, and hence the properties cannot be changed, or some field values are disabled. You can unlock the control by clicking the lock icon under the **Advanced** section for the corresponding control.

5. Let's now look at some of the controls that are doing the action on this screen. Let's start with **TopBar_RightContainer1** and you will see a number of button controls, including **IconButton_Accept1**, **IconButton_Cancel1**, and **IconButton_Edit1**.

6. Let's pick the first button, **IconButton_Accept1**, and see the different properties. The default property that gets shown on the top is **OnSelect**, which determines how the app responds when the control is selected.

    Here, the value is set to a function call as **SubmitForm (EditForm1)**, which is a standard function used in Power Apps to save changes on the form elements into the data source (the Dataverse table, in this example). If you are unable to see the actual control, that is because it might be hidden in the default view. You can change the drop-down value from **OnSelect** to **Visible**, as shown in the following screenshot:

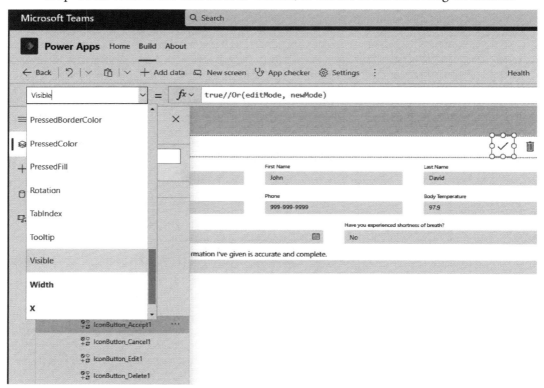

Figure 3.23 – Visible property on controls

As seen in the snapshot, the value for this property is **Or(editMode, newMode)**. However, I changed it to **true**, just to make it visible for illustration. This means that the visibility of this control was earlier set to be based on the evaluation of this function, **Or(editMode, newMode)**, which will evaluate to true only when the form is in **editMode** or **newMode**. Now, if you quickly glance at the buttons for **New record** (**TouchTarget_New1** in **LeftControlContainer1**) or **IconButton_Edit1**, you will realize that the values for these variables, **editMode** and **newMode**, are set to true when selecting a new record or editing existing ones. All this logic was already pre-configured, and you can easily change it in the same way as modifying formulas in Microsoft Excel.

Information about variables

Variables (such as **editMode** and **newMode**) are used to hold a value and pass context between the screens. As seen in the earlier example, you can set the values to be true or false based on a condition, and then use this information in another screen to modify the behavior of any screen or control elements. You can see all the variables that are created or the ones you create by clicking the **Settings** icon.

Also, you will have noticed that within **LeftContainer1**, there is a **BrowseGallery1** field, which is like a list of all the records that are present in the table or newly entered values from the app. This list or collection of values is rendered using a **Gallery** control and, in this example, if you look at the properties of this control, it has pre-selected a view that has one icon image and two text values (**Image1**, **Subtitle1**, and **Title1** fields in the screenshot). This can be modified using the **Layout** properties of this control, as shown in the following screenshot:

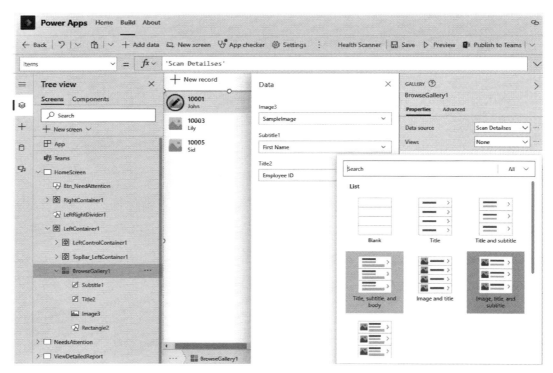

Figure 3.24 – Layouts for the Gallery control

In the options shown in the preceding screenshot, we will be choosing the **Title, subtitle, and body** option since we don't need any image/thumbnail type data to be displayed.

Now, as you can see in the following screenshot, we can get the desired fields to be shown in the gallery view:

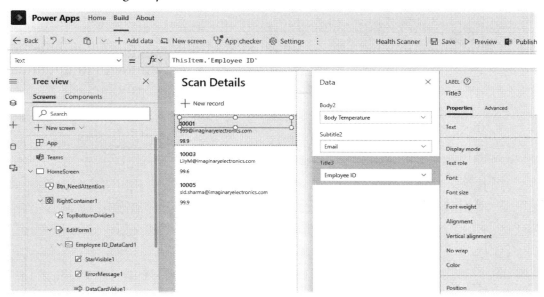

Figure 3.25 – Customizing fields in the Gallery layout

You now have a working app that can take inputs and store them in a secure place, from where they can be retrieved when required. In the next sub-section, we will see how this can be further customized to suit the requirements of the business.

Customizing the app

In this section, we will see how we can customize this app to solve a critical business problem that we wanted to tackle, in other words, to identify employees with a body temperature in excess of 99 degrees Fahrenheit who need to be quarantined due to health concerns. In such cases, you would need to have a filtered view across all the employees and be able to quickly determine such employees who need to be quarantined. Follow these instructions to do this:

1. To do this, we will make use of some real estate on the right side of this screen. We will first resize the **RightContainer1** field to make some space on the right-hand side of the screen.

2. Next, as shown in the following screenshot, using the + icon to insert screen elements, add a new vertical container called **Container4**:

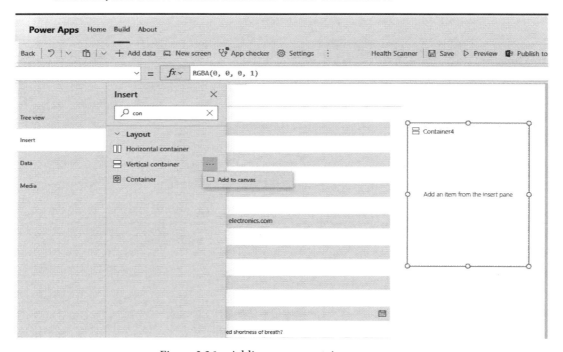

Figure 3.26 – Adding a new container on screen

3. Next, we will rename it RightMarginContainer using the **Screens Tree view** in the editing panel to the left:

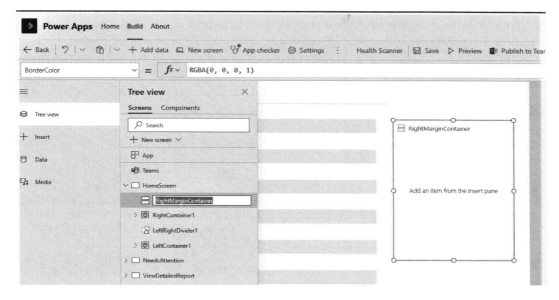

Figure 3.27 – Renaming a container from the Screens Tree view

4. Using the same **Add option** field from the left pane, we will add another label and **Vertical gallery**. The label will hold the text for the title of this container and the gallery will show the list of employees that need attention. As soon as you add the gallery, you will be prompted to choose the data source, which is the **Scan Details** table in our case. You can see in the following screenshot how this will appear on your screen, and then, using the properties for resizing the gallery, you can adjust it to fit the size of the container and screen:

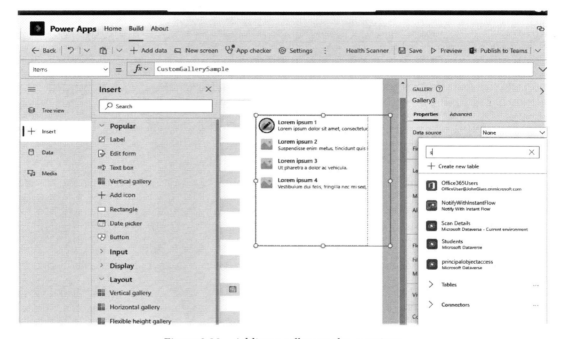

Figure 3.28 – Adding a gallery to the container

While adding the gallery and labels to the container, ensure that you have selected the container control while adding the gallery. This ensures that the label and gallery controls are correctly aligned under the container element in the Screens Tree view hierarchy.

5. Next, we will add a label as a title to the gallery. The label width and font can be adjusted using the **Properties** pane, very much like changing the fonts on a Microsoft Word document. As seen in the following screenshot, the font color and text should be modified to say Needs Attention:

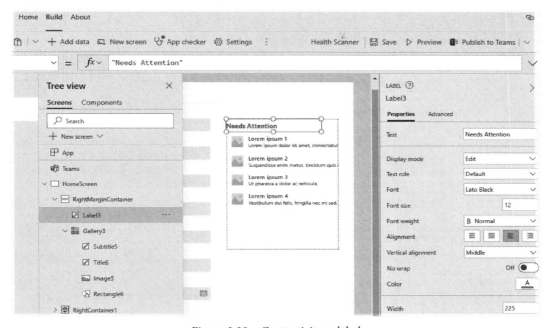

Figure 3.29 – Customizing a label

Now, you will notice that the list of employees in the gallery is still the same since we haven't applied any business logic to filter out the employees who meet the quarantine criterion, in other words, a body temperature in excess of 99 degrees Fahrenheit.

6. We will select **Gallery Item** in the new container and select the **Items** property in the dropdown, as shown in the following screenshot. Meanwhile, we can rename this gallery to Needs Attention and change the color to highlight it using the properties on the right side of your screen, as shown in the following screenshot:

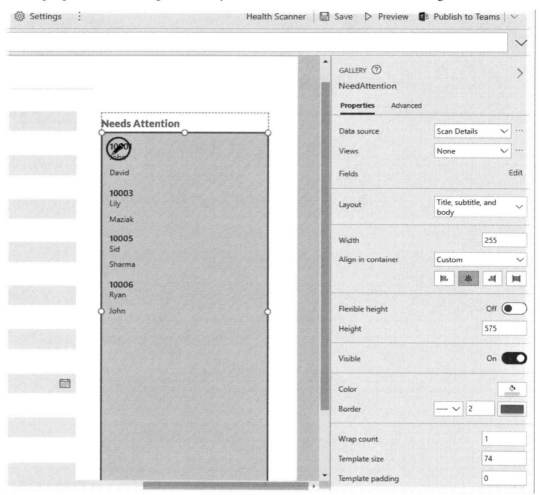

Figure 3.30 – Gallery properties in Power Apps

Here, in the **Items** property, you will notice that all the values in the **Scan Details** table are currently listed in the gallery. This needs to be filtered to just show the employees that need attention.

7. To add this filter to the gallery items, you will use the built-in function in Power Apps called **Filter**. So, instead of **Scan Details**, you will change this value to `Filter('Scan Details','Body Temperature' >99)`, as shown in the following screenshot:

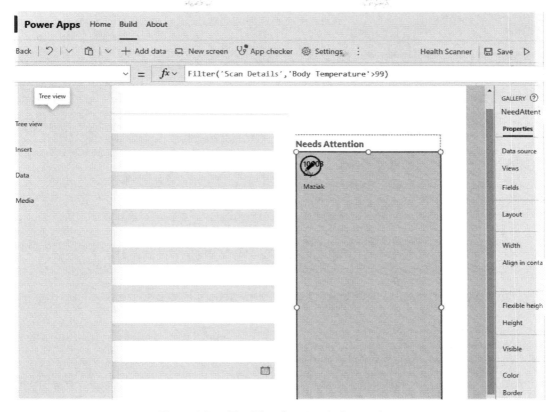

Figure 3.31 – The Filter function in Power Apps

The IntelliSense prompt from the platform will show the expected formula definition and helps you to know that the **Filter** function expects two parameters – the source to which the filter is applied, and the logical test to evaluate or filter the criterion to be applied to all records within the source. In our case, this source is the **Scan Details** table, and the filter criterion is a body temperature above 99 degrees Fahrenheit, which is expressed as a mathematical expression in the logical test.

Important Note

Comments can be written inline into formulas to help improve the readability of the formulas. These comments help you to maintain the application over the lifetime of an application. Comments can be added in a single line using two forward slashes (//) or in a multi-line comments format using the forward slash and asterisk (/ and *) together. The forward slash followed by an asterisk is used to start the comments, and an asterisk followed by a forward slash is used to close the comments. For example, `/* your comments go here*/`. These comments are ignored by Power Apps for evaluation or computation, and can be viewed as dead code, left there simply for our convenience.

As soon as you finish the filter formula, you will see that the **Needs Attention** gallery is now filtered to just show the records where the body temperature of the employee (Lily, as in the example in the preceding screenshot) was recorded to be over 99.9 F. To test this further, I added another record for a new employee (Ryan) with a temperature recording of 99.1 F and this immediately shows up in the **Needs Attention** gallery.

8. Once you think all your functionality required in the application is complete, you should use the built-in **App checker** (see the top menu under the Power Apps Main menu) to fix some of the common errors and accessibility issues. As seen in the following screenshot, I am missing **AccessibleLabel** for some of the controls that were added while customizing the app:

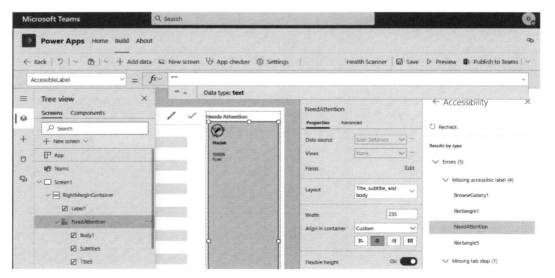

Figure 3.32 – Filter function in Power Apps

AccessibleLabel helps people with visual impairments who use screen narrator software to read out the text provided on screen. When the mouse hovers over any control, this value for **AccessibleLabel** is read out by the narrator. More information about how to make your applications accessible can be found here: `https://docs.microsoft.com/en-us/powerapps/maker/canvas-apps/accessible-apps`.

Health Scanner is now ready to be tested and published for consumption. To publish the application, you will use the **Publish to Teams** option in the top-right corner of your screen. Once you click this option, you will be prompted with the following screenshot:

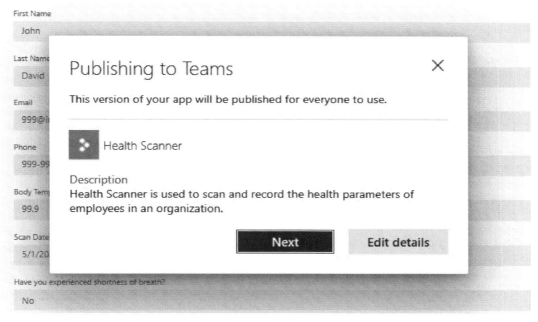

Figure 3.33 – Publishing an app to Teams

9. Using **Edit Details**, you can get to the option where you add a description and custom icon for your application. For the **Health Scanner** application, I chose a custom icon of a stethoscope and added a description, as seen in the following screenshot:

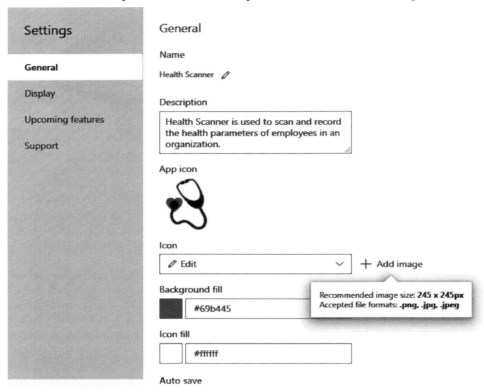

Figure 3.34 – Adding an app icon and description

10. Once you have updated these, there are a few more properties, such as screen size and other advanced settings, that you can play with. Click the back arrow to go back to your app and click the **Publish to Teams** button, followed by the **Next** button to continue publishing your application. As seen in the following screenshot, this will prompt you to choose a channel with your existing team:

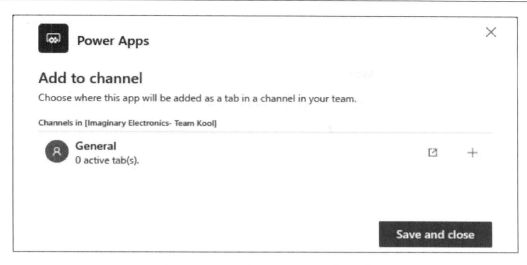

Figure 3.35 – Adding an app to a channel

Additionally, you can navigate to the **General** Teams channel and use the + icon
in the menu to pin this app to this general channel or a new channel as needed.
More information about the Teams channel can be found here: `https://docs.`
`microsoft.com/en-us/microsoftteams/teams-channels-overview`.

I created a new channel with the name **Health Scan Recordings** under the team and
then added the **Health Scanner** application, as shown in the following screenshot:

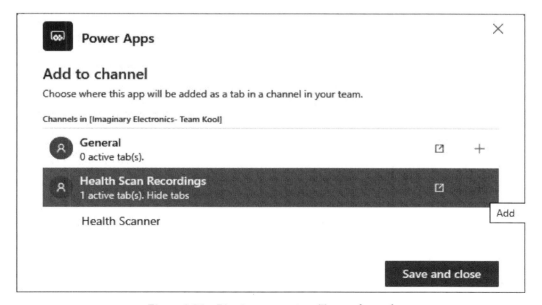

Figure 3.36 – Pinning an app to a Teams channel

The Health Scanner app is now ready for use by all members of the team! You can navigate to the Teams channel (**Health Scan Recordings**) and view the application:

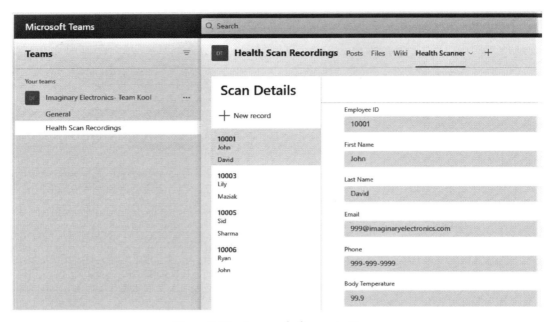

Figure 3.37 – App ready for use in Teams

You have just finished building your first application – **Health Scanner** – without writing any lines of code and just one formula for the **Filter** function. You can build many other such applications based on the business scenarios that might arise in your organization. In this section, we learned about the basic elements of Power Apps and how a screen can be built with fields and customized to apply business rules. An exhaustive list of all formulas available in Power Apps can be found at this link: https://docs.microsoft.com/en-us/powerapps/maker/canvas-apps/formula-reference.

Summary

In this chapter, you have learned how to build a table in Microsoft Dataverse for Teams and build an app from scratch. You have also seen how various elements of Power Apps are used to build an app. To summarize, let's look at some of the important elements of the app that you learned in this chapter. The **Health Scanner** app had a table where data was stored. These tables are stored in Dataverse for Teams, something that we learned in the previous chapter. Next, we learned about how a screen has various elements that are added to this screen. Within the screen, you were able to insert a **Gallery**, which helped you to display all the records. You also learned how a **Form** is used to edit the data records or insert new records into the table. While customizing the app, you were also able to easily modify the properties of various screen elements. You also learned how formulas work, which enabled you to add a new gallery that filtered records to match your business needs.

In the next chapter, we will take a deeper look at Microsoft Dataverse for Teams and some of the advanced functionalities that can be added to the **Health Scanner** app.

4
Enhancing Your App with Images, Screens, and File Attachments

In the previous chapter, we learned to build our first application, **Health Scanner**, using Microsoft Dataverse. In this chapter, we will learn some more advanced topics of Dataverse and apply them to enhance the **Health Scanner** application.

We will begin by looking at some post-publishing details, such as handling different application versions, usage analytics, and then adding additional information that would be needed in this application (for example, adding detailed reports and a profile picture in relation to any employee).

The important topics that will be covered are as follows:

- Application Versions and Analytics
- Adding multiple screens to your application

- Establishing a relationship between the tables
- Adding images and related records to your application

Let's begin by looking at different versions of the app and how they help in application publishing. Then we'll look at some analytics that are provided automatically by the platform; these analytics will help you derive insights on how your application is being used.

Application Versions and Analytics

Application versions help you to keep track of changes and manage these changes better. For example, once you release version 1.0 of your app and it goes live, you can start working on version 2.0 and introducing new features, as we are about to start doing in the next topic in this chapter. Meanwhile, while doing so, we will also want to see how version 1.0 is doing with respect to usage. As an app owner or a product owner invested in the success of your app, you will need to monitor some key usage metrics, such as the number of daily active users of your application. In the next few steps, let's take a look at how we can see these analytics:

1. To begin, let's start by opening the **Build** hub. As seen in the following screenshot, you can navigate to the editing experience of the app again:

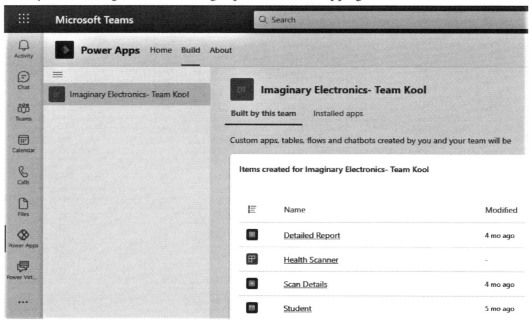

Figure 4.1 – Build hub view

2. Additionally, if you click the **See all** link, you get to see more details of the app, including versions and usage analytics.

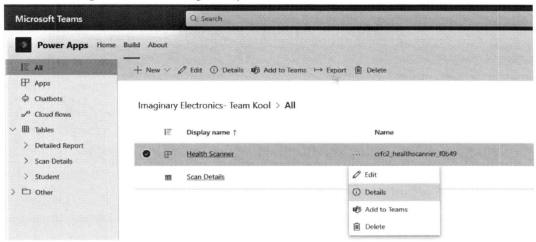

Figure 4.2 – Build hub details

3. When clicking on the details, you will see the different options (tabs) by means of which you can navigate to see the analytics (usage). Here, you will see the number of apps launched by day, their daily active users, and so on.

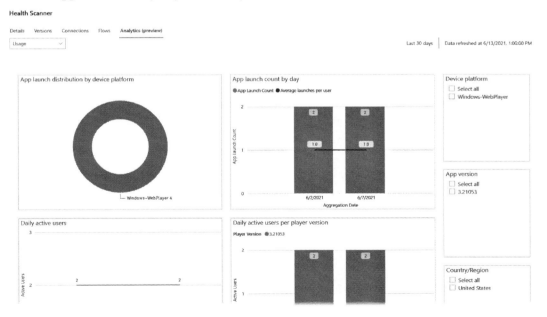

Figure 4.3 – Analytics on application usage

4.   Similarly, under the **Versions** menu option (tab), you can see, as in the following screenshot, different versions that were created, including the version that is currently **Live**:

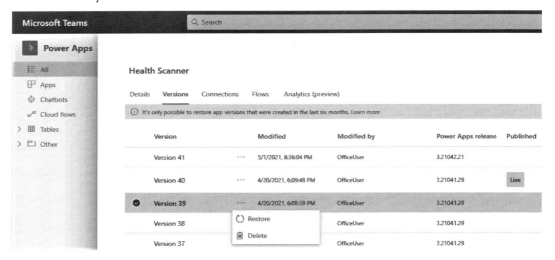

Figure 4.4 – Versioning of applications

In the preceding screenshot, you can see that you can make any of the previous versions **Live** as well. This is usually done when a recently published live version is reported to have bugs and you would like to roll back and make the previous stable version as the live version that end users can use. This is usually required so that end users can conduct business while you get time to debug and fix the latest version. The rollback is done by picking the stable version and clicking **Restore**, as shown in the preceding screenshot. This will ensure that the version that is restored becomes the live version that end users of the application will be able to use once restoration is complete.

Similarly, there are some other sections here, such as **Connections** and **Flows**. If your app connects to additional data sources, they will be listed under **Connections**, and if your app incorporates any Power Automate flows, they will be listed under **Flows**.

In the next section, we will start working on the next version of the application to add multiple screens that will focus on different scenarios within the **Health Scanner** application.

Adding multiple screens to your application

In previous chapters, you might have observed that all the operations were being performed on the same screen. In this topic, we will try to segregate the scenarios into different screens; for example, the view where you can see employees who need attention can be on a different screen, since this view needs to be seen only by a select few of the audience, such as managers or doctors in the organization:

1. Open the **Health Scanner** app from the **Build** hub.

2. Click on **Screen1** and rename it to HomeScreen. This will help us to differentiate between the scenarios and relate them to the appropriate screens.

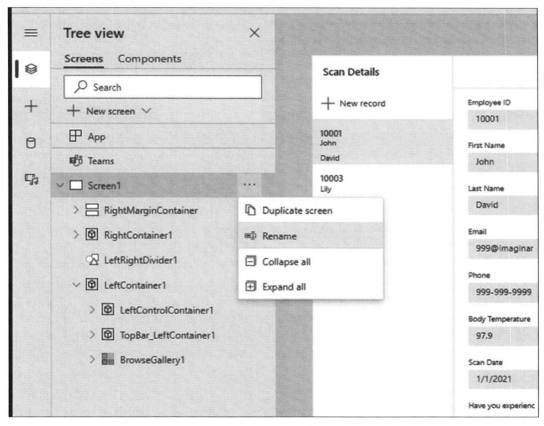

Figure 4.5 – Renaming Screen1 to HomeScreen

3. Insert another new screen, using the **New Screen** option above the tree view hierarchy, as shown in the following screenshot. While doing so, you will see different types of layouts; choose the **Sidebar** option.

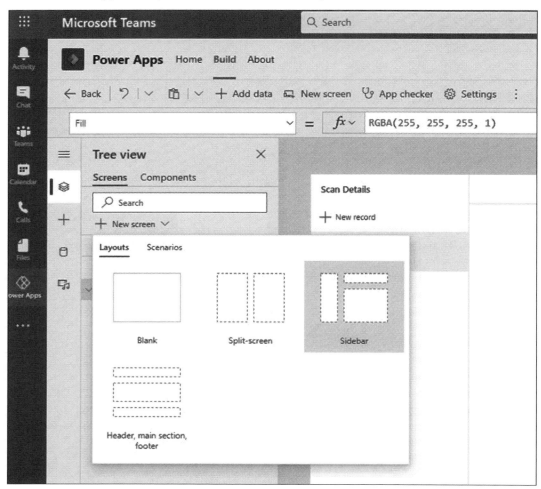

Figure 4.6 – Inserting a new screen

This option just helps us with pre-defined containers based on the layout we plan for our new screen. Similarly, you will see that right next to the **Layouts** option, there is an option to pre-select some scenarios. These are screen layouts focused on scenarios such as Email, People, and Meeting. Choosing these layouts helps with an ideal layout that end users of your application would expect for dealing with these scenarios and saves you some time while building and laying out controls. For example, choosing the **People** scenario type would automatically make the new screen layout look like a people search or directory, where users would look up information about other colleagues in the organization.

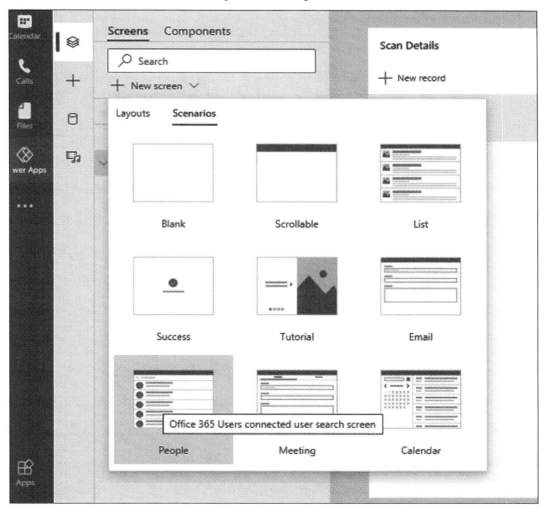

Figure 4.7 – Layouts and scenarios available for New screen

4. Now you can just navigate to **HomeScreen**, copy **RightMarginContainer**, and paste it on **Screen2**. As seen in the following screenshot, you will see that the container is now on the new screen – **Screen2**:

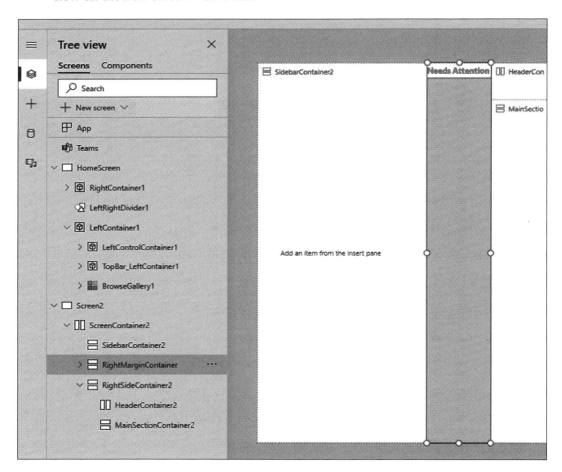

Figure 4.8 – Pasting containers on a new screen

After pasting the RightMarginContainer to the new screen, we can delete it from the Homescreen as we will be adding button there, as seen in the following steps.

5. Now you can delete **SidebarContainer2** and rename **RightMarginContainer** to `LeftMarginContainer2` to appropriately depict the new orientation of this container within the new screen. Then you can use the width property of the containers to adjust the width and layouts on the screens, as seen in the following screenshot:

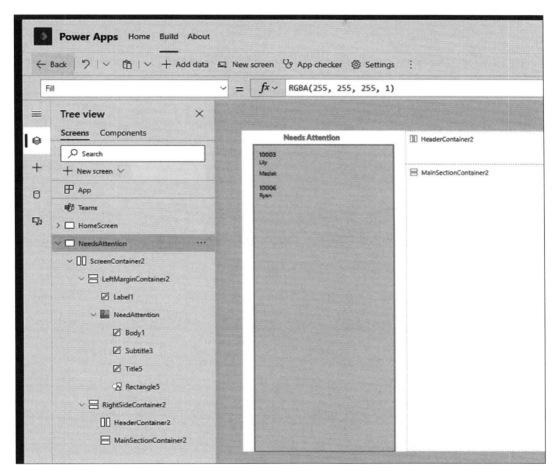

Figure 4.9 – Realigning containers on the new screen

6. Let's rename **Screen2** as `NeedsAttention`. Next, we will add a detailed employee scanning report on this page to analyze these cases further.

7. As seen in the following screenshot, using the **Insert** button, let's add a **Label** and change the Text property to say **Detailed Report**:

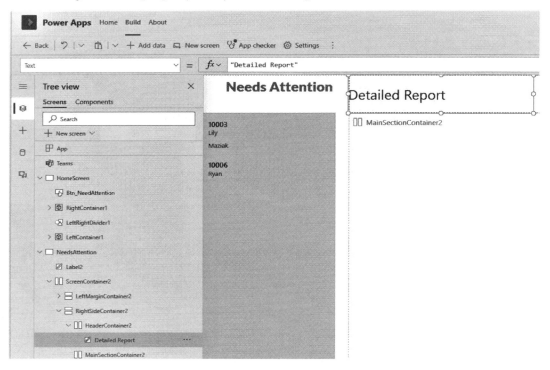

Figure 4.10 – Adding a header label

8. Next, let's add a new label, **Full Name**, to **HeaderContainer2**, as seen in the following screenshot. Additionally, change the **Text** property of this label to `Concatenate(NeedAttention.Selected.'First Name', " ", NeedAttention.Selected.'Last Name')`.

This will ensure that the full name of the employee appears on the screen. You can also see how two fields can be concatenated for display purposes. In this formula, we see that the selected values (**First Name** and **Last Name**) from the **NeedAttention** gallery are concatenated. This changes the text based on the selection on the left gallery control, in other words, the label changes based on the employee (Lily or Ryan) that is selected in the left gallery.

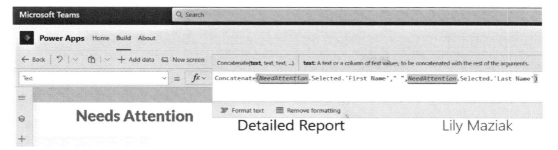

Figure 4.11 – Adding a full name label

9. You can adjust the font size and height of the label using the Label properties on the right side of the screen. Using the **Height** and **Width** properties of the controls, adjust the layout of controls within the container.

10. Since **MainSectionContainer2** is a vertical container, you will observe that the layout of the controls is always vertically aligned, one below the other. We will change this to be horizontally aligned by changing the **Direction** property dropdown of **MainSectionContainer2** on the right-hand pane to **Horizontal**.

    If you wish to learn more about the containers and various layouts, you will find more information at this link: https://docs.microsoft.com/en-us/powerapps/maker/canvas-apps/build-responsive-apps.

11. Now, let's build the connection and navigation between the two screens. Add a button control to **Home Screen**, move it to the right side of all the containers, and rename it `Btn_NeedAttention`, as shown in the following screenshot. Change the **Text** property of the button to **Employees Needing Attention** and then, finally, in the OnSelect property, provide the Navigate function as `Navigate(NeedsAttention)`. This will ensure that when you click on this button, the **NeedsAttention** screen will be loaded.

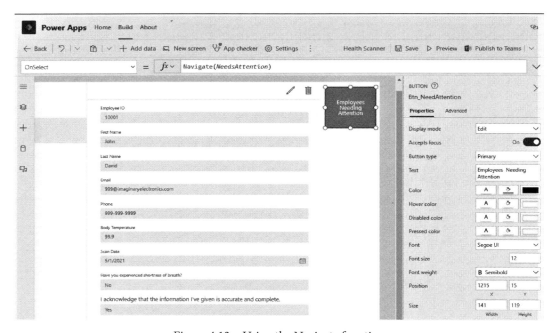

Figure 4.12 – Using the Navigate function

In the next section, we will see how we can add an image column (profile picture) to an existing table. Also, we will see how to establish a relationship between two tables that contain related records, for example, how to store additional records related to employees, in a different related table.

Establishing a relationship between the tables

In this section, we will add a new table to store detailed reports and add a profile picture for the employee in the **Scan Details** table that was used to show records on **HomeScreen**:

1. To start with, let's save the changes done in the app so far and navigate back to the **Build** hub. Here you can navigate to the table details using **Build | Team Name (Imaginary Electronics- Team Kool) | Built by this team | Scan Details**.

    Once you land on the table details page, as seen in the following screenshot, you can add a column of the **Image** data type:

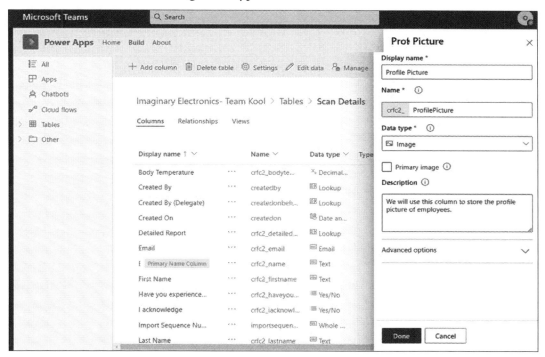

Figure 4.13 – Adding an Image column to the table

We will use this column to store the profile picture of the employee.

2. Following this, let's create a new table, **Detailed Report**, to store the detailed report of the employees. While creating this table, you will need to understand that each row in this new table will be storing a document specific to each employee.

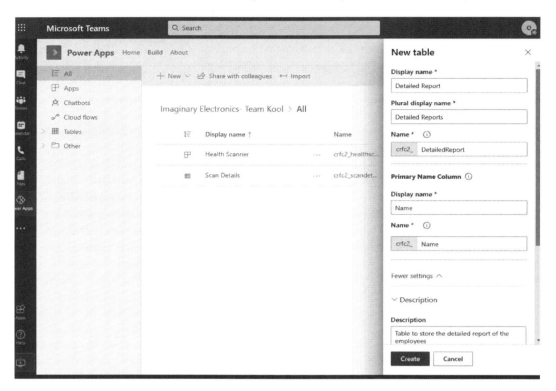

Figure 4.14 – Creating a new table from the Build hub

This new table will need two columns – **Employee ID** (such as the primary name column in the **Scan Details** table) and **Report**. If you observe the following screenshot, you will observe that instead of creating a new field for **Employee ID**, I changed the display name for the existing **crfc2_name**, which is **Primary Name Column**:

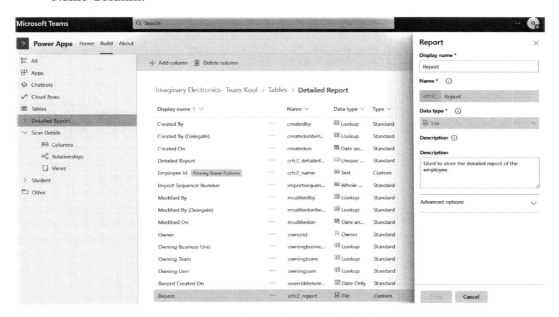

Figure 4.15 – Adding a column of the File data type

3. Now, let's go back to the **Scan Details** table and establish the link with this newly created table, **Detailed Report**. This building of a relationship between tables is part of data modeling using entity relations between the tables, as we will see in *Chapter 5, Understanding Microsoft Dataverse*, in the *Relational data* section.

4. Select the **Relationships** section in **Scan Details** and click the **Add relationship** option. Here, we are going to select the **Many-to-one** relationship.

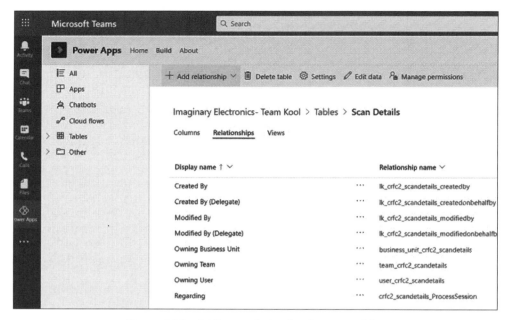

Figure 4.16 – Adding a relationship between tables

The many-to-one type is chosen to represent the type of relationship between these tables; in other words, many scan details, based on different dates, will still point to one, and only one, detailed report per employee.

5. Next, as seen in the following screenshot, choose the **Detailed Report** table:

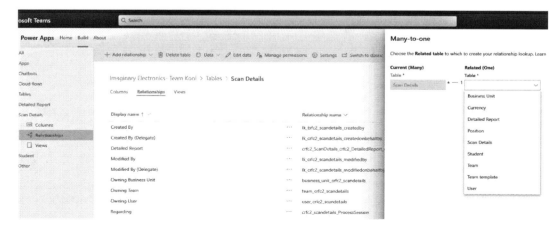

Figure 4.17 – Creating a many-to-one relationship between tables

6. Once the table is chosen, you will get the option to change the column name, which will be used to look up the corresponding detailed report.

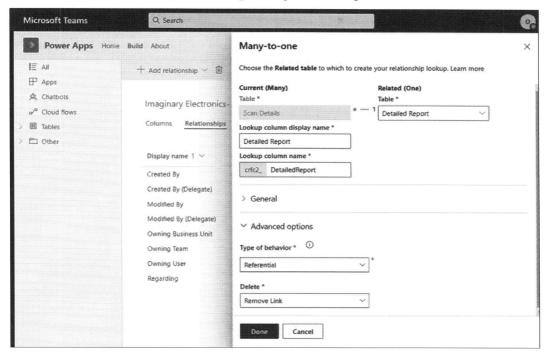

Figure 4.18 – Lookup column name

As seen in the preceding screenshot, we will use a simple **Referential** type of behavior. You can create a lookup column directly, which will help you generate this relationship automatically as outlined in the documentation: `https://docs.microsoft.com/en-us/powerapps/maker/data-platform/data-platform-entity-lookup`. As seen in this preceding documentation, Dataverse also supports different types of behavior for establishing relationships between tables.

In the next section, we will see how to continue to add image controls and wire them up to the tables.

Adding images and related records to your application

In this section, first, we will see how to add the profile picture to the employee's scan records and then see how to get related detailed records of the employee on the linked screen, which has a list of employees needing attention:

1. On **Home Screen**, for the **Edit form** control, edit the field under **EditForm1** properties and add the **Profile Picture** field, as shown in the following screenshot:

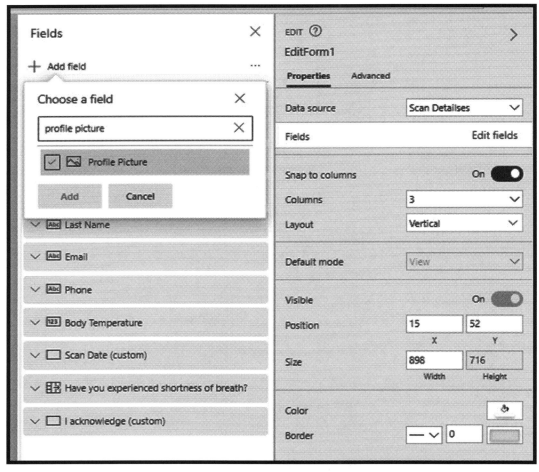

Figure 4.19 – Adding an Image field to the form

2. Next, using the three dots (...) on the field property, you can move this newly added **Profile Picture** field and related control to the top of the form, as seen in the following screenshot:

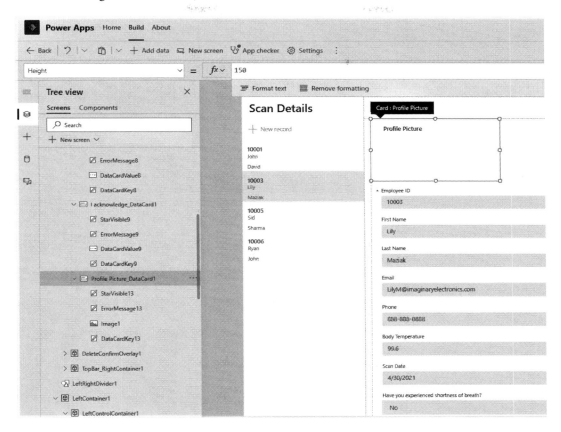

Figure 4.20 – Adding an Image field within the Edit Form control

3. Once this is done, you can test this control and navigation by using the **Preview** option. In the following screenshot, you can see that I was able to add a profile picture for an employee, using the control, and testing the navigation to the **Needs Attention** screen:

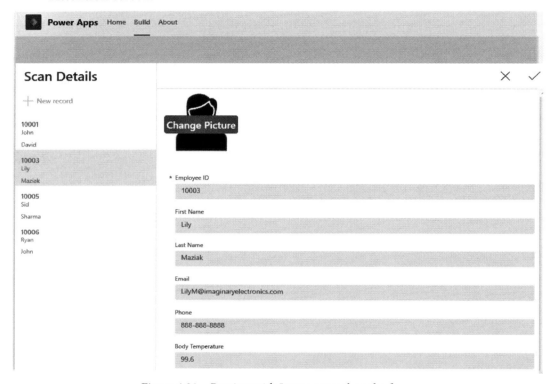

Figure 4.21 – Preview with Image control on the form

4. You can use this form to add profile pictures for all employees, using the **Tap or click to add a picture** button, which is autogenerated when you add a field of the **Image** type to the form. It is important to note that images, such as profile pictures in this example, cannot be edited through the table editor experience.

5. Now, let's go to the **Needs Attention** screen and add two controls – **Vertical gallery** and **Edit form**. We will use the gallery to list all the related detailed reports, while **Edit form** will be used to add more detailed reports related to the employee, if needed. We will name the gallery **DetailedReportGallery** and the form NewDetailedReportForm.

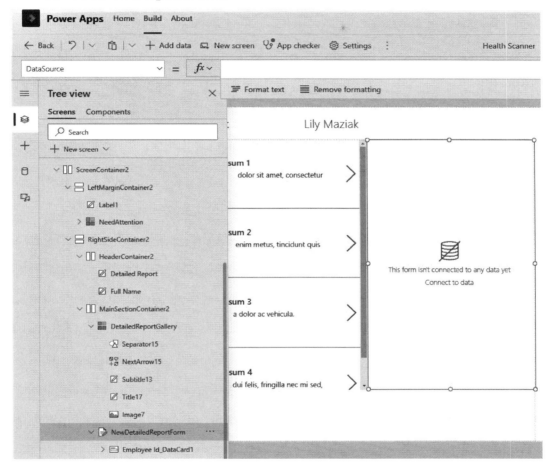

Figure 4.22 – Adding a vertical gallery and edit form to the screen

6. Let's wire **DetailedReportGallery** to show the corresponding reports of the employee, who is selected in the **NeedsAttention** gallery inside **LeftMarginContainer2**. Update the **Items** property of the gallery to `Filter('Detailed Reports','Employee Id'= NeedAttention.Selected.'Employee ID')`.

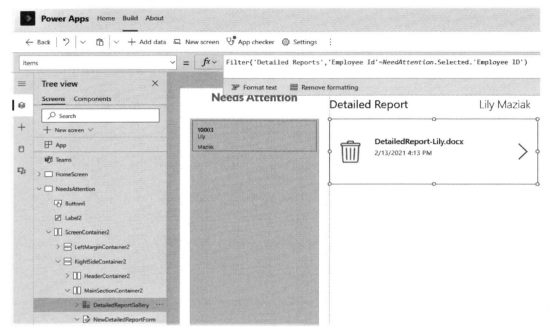

Figure 4.23 – Adding a vertical gallery and edit form to the screen

Since we don't yet have any detailed reports uploaded, it will not show any items in the gallery.

Under the gallery hierarchy, you will see a rectangular control that covers the border around each item in the gallery. This border can be made more distinct using border properties such as types (dotted, dashed, or bold line), thickness (numeric value), and the color of the border. As seen in the preceding screenshot, let's change the thickness to 1 and give it some subtle color of your choice. You can also change the background color of the gallery item if you wish to.

7. Next, let's wire up the form so that we can provide an option for users to add detailed reports. Update the **Data source** property of the form to connect to the **Detailed Reports** table and add the **Employee Id** and **Report** fields. You will see that the **Report** field made the app automatically add an attachment control to the form.

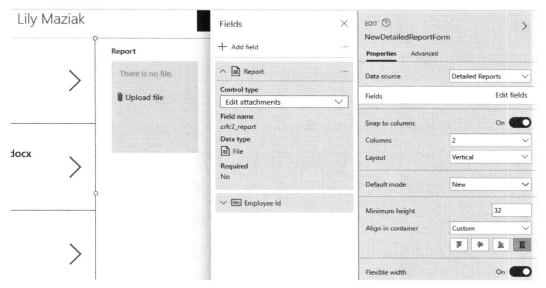

Figure 4.24 – Connecting the form to a data source

8. Now, the last thing to add to this screen is a button that will help you to submit the form, in other words, the new detailed report can be uploaded to the table. This can be done by updating the OnSelect property of the button with `SubmitForm`, with the value as `SubmitForm(NewDetailedReportForm)`. Modify the **Text** property to say **Add Report**, and format other properties such as **Border** and **Color** as required.

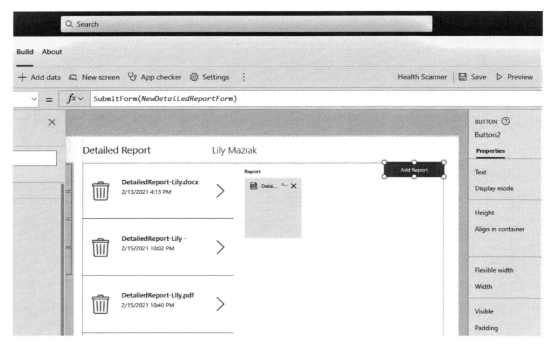

Figure 4.25 – Adding a button to submit the form

Similarly, for the form to be visible, every time it is loaded, we will add the value `NewForm(NewDetailedReportForm)` for all properties, including **OnSuccess**, **OnFailure**, and **OnReset**. This ensures that every time there is a failure, success, or reset, a new form will be presented on the screen.

Update the **Item** property of the form with the value
`If(DetailedReportGallery.DisplayMode = DisplayMode.`
`Disabled, DetailedReportGallery.Selected,`
`DetailedReportGallery.Selected)`. The form will not be visible in
Preview mode unless the **Item** property is set.

You can also set the **DefaultMode** property of the form to **New**, which will just
show a new form as the default.

9. Use Preview mode for testing. Using the **Add Report** button on the form, add
    a detailed report (I have used Word and PDF files as samples in the following
    screenshots):

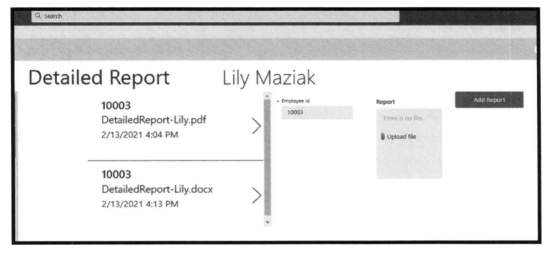

Figure 4.26 – Preview with detailed reports added

Here, you will observe that the **Add Report** button being visible all the time allows
users to be able to add records without the need for a file to be uploaded through
the control. To prevent this, let's set the **Visible** property of the button to the
following value:

`If(IsEmpty(DataCardValue12.Attachments.Value),false,true)`

This will ensure that the button will become visible only when a user selects a report
file using the attachment control.

10. As seen in the preceding screenshot, **Employee Id** is repeated every item for **DetailedReportGallery**, which can be fixed by changing the **Layout** property of the gallery to the **Image, title, and subtitle** type, and by changing **Fields** to just show the **SampleImage, Report.File Name**, and **Created On** fields.

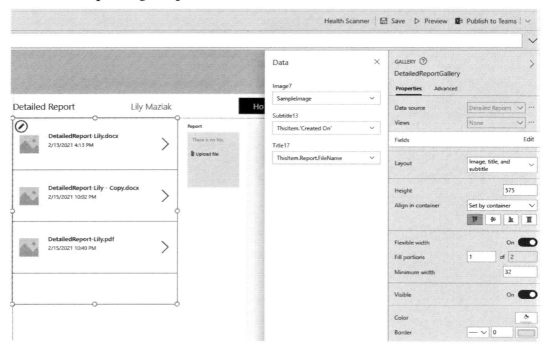

Figure 4.27 – Changing the layout of the gallery

11. We will use the **SampleImage** field to upload a delete/trash icon that can be used to directly delete unwanted or old reports, if needed. Using the **Image** property of the image, as shown in the following screenshot, we will add this trash icon, which will be used as a button to remove items from the gallery:

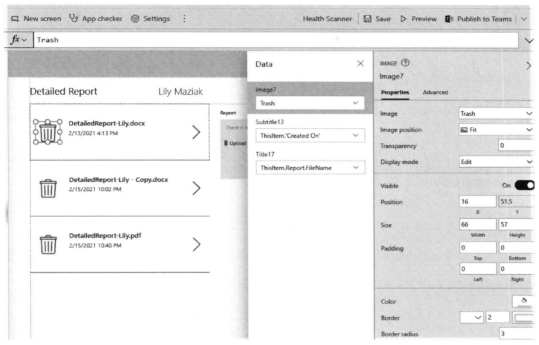

Figure 4.28 – Changing the sample image in the gallery

As seen in the following screenshot, using the **OnSelect** property of the image at the top of the screen, we will now update the value to use the Remove('Detailed Reports',DetailedReportGallery.Selected) function.

This will help us to remove the selected item from the **Detailed Reports** table, thereby helping the user to remove an unwanted detailed report or an incorrect file that was uploaded.

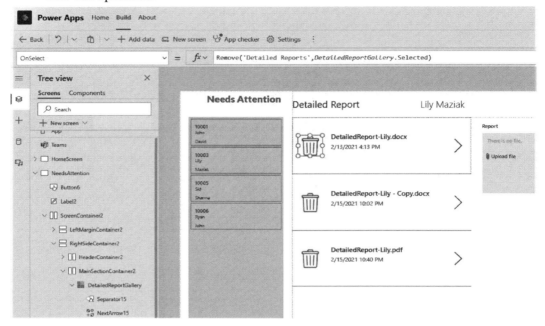

Figure 4.29 – Removing items from a gallery

12. Since the **Employee Id** value is something that we won't be changing, but is a required field for the form to be updated, it is better to hide this data card. This can be done by updating the **Visible** property of **Data Card** for **Employee Id** to **false**.

13. We will now need to add a third screen to our app, which will be used for viewing the details of each gallery item and deleting them, if necessary. This approach can be used for every situation where a gallery item needs to be viewed with all the fields in that item record and subsequent actions performed, such as editing or deletion. Using the **New Screen** button at the top of the function bar (the place where property values or functions are provided), let's add the following new screen, **ViewDetailedReport**.

14. Next, we need to update the **OnSelect** property of the **NextArrow** icon of the **DetailedReportGallery** gallery on the **Needs Attention** screen with the value `Navigate(ViewDetailedReport)`. This will assist with navigation to this newly created **ViewDetailedReport** screen.

15. On this new screen, let's add two controls – a label with the name **Employee Name**, which will serve as a screen header, showing the name of the employee whose record is being viewed, and an edit form with the name **EmployeeDetailedReportForm**:

```
Concatenate("Detailed Report For Employee :
",NeedAttention.Selected.'First Name'," ",NeedAttention.
Selected.'Last Name')
```

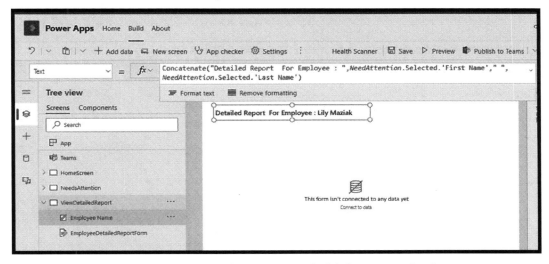

Figure 4.30 – Creating dynamic text in the label as a screen header

16. Now, using the **Data source** property on **EmployeeDetailedReportForm**, we can connect the form to the **Detailed Reports** table. Next, as seen in the following screenshot, we need to update the **Item** property of the form to point to the selected item from **DetailedReportGallery**; in other words, the detailed report version that was selected on the previous screen gets rendered. We also need to add the **Created On** field to this form to match the fields that were displayed on the gallery, and also to track the version of the report that is being rendered. The **Employee Id** field can be removed as this is implicit and doesn't need to be updated, nor is it required, since the employee's name is available in the label that we generated previously as part of the screen header.

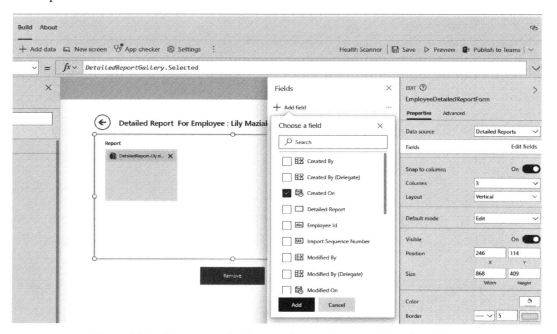

Figure 4.31 – Connecting the form to show a select item from the gallery

17. Next, we will add a button, **RemoveDetailedReport**, to remove/delete this record, if needed. As seen in the following screenshot, you can change the color to some shade of red, just to signify that it is a non-reversible delete action, while placement of the button can be adjusted appropriately. The **OnSelect** property of the button is updated with the following value:

```
Remove('Detailed Reports',DetailedReportGallery.Selected)
```

This will cause the records to be removed from the table when this button is pressed.

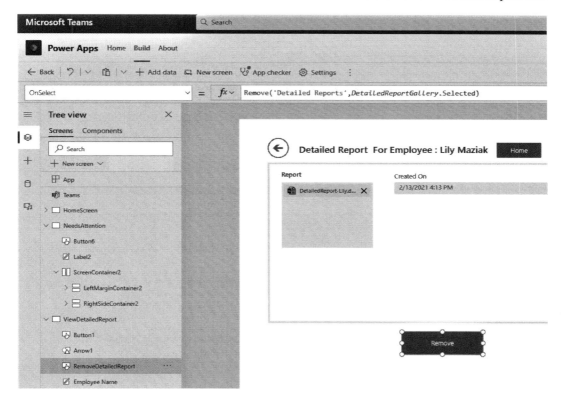

Figure 4.32 – Removing the function used with a button to delete records

18. Next, we can add two button controls; first, a back button or **Arrow** icon to help us navigate back to the **Needs Attention** screen, and a second button for navigating back to the home screen directly from this screen. As can be seen in the following screenshot, you can update the **OnSelect** properties of these buttons using the **Navigate** function and target the appropriate screens. You can adjust the alignments, color, and font size of the screen elements to provide the final touches to this screen.

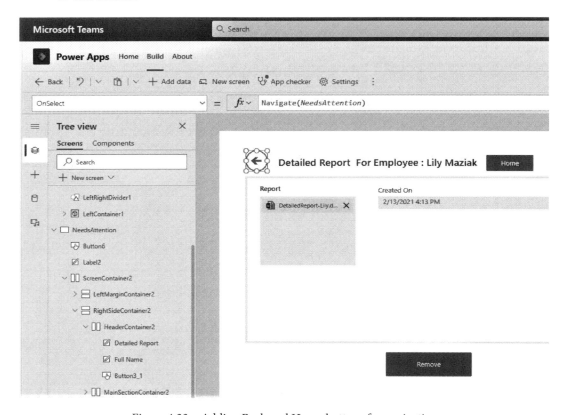

Figure 4.33 – Adding Back and Home buttons for navigation

The same **Home** button can be copied and pasted to the **Needs Attention** screen under **HeaderContainer2**, as seen in the following screenshot, so that there is a navigation option to **HomeScreen** from the **Needs Attention** screen as well.

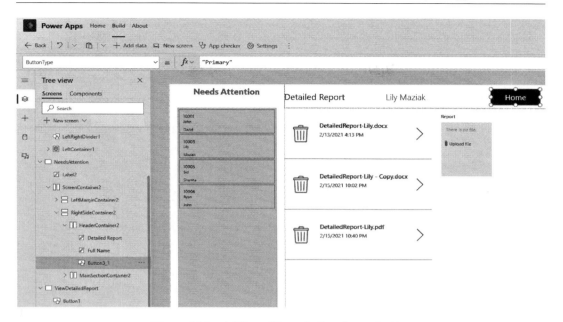

Figure 4.34 – Adding a Home button for navigation

Now your app is ready for business, and using the preview feature, you can insert profile pictures for all employees and detailed reports for employees requiring attention. This app is now ready to be published to the Teams channel, just like we published the initial version toward the end of *Chapter 3, Building Your First App with Microsoft Dataverse for Teams*.

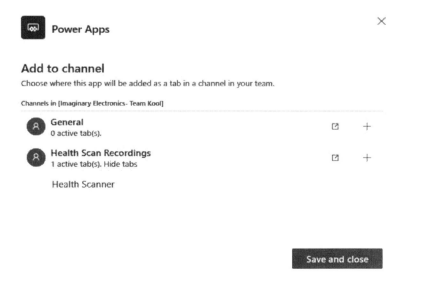

Figure 4.35 – Publishing your app to the Teams channel

In this section, you learned how to build controls to support **Image** and **File** data types. You also learned how to build forms that can help you update and delete records containing image and file data types from a table.

Summary

In this chapter, you were able to enhance your first application to support complex data types such as Image and File data types. Additionally, you were able to build a relationship of the one-to-many type between different tables and learned how to build forms to update and delete such records. You also learned about the analytics of your apps and how you can use them to learn more about how your app is being used by users.

In the next chapter, we will explore Microsoft Dataverse in more detail. This is a fully loaded data platform that can help you to build and run applications outside of the Teams environment, if necessary.

Section 2: Deep Dive into Microsoft Dataverse for Teams

To build rock-solid applications that meet the enterprise requirements of secure and reliable storage with a strong governance model, it is imperative that you find a reliable data platform. Microsoft Dataverse is that platform. It easily structures a variety of data and business logic to support interconnected applications and processes in a secure and compliant manner. In this section, you will learn more about Microsoft Dataverse, besides building your first Power Automate flow and Power Virtual Agents bot.

This section comprises the following chapters:

- *Chapter 5, Understanding Microsoft Dataverse*
- *Chapter 6, Automating with Microsoft Dataverse for Teams*
- *Chapter 7, Building Power Virtual Agents Bots with Microsoft Dataverse for Teams*

5
Understanding Microsoft Dataverse

In the previous chapter, we learned how to augment an application with complex data types such as files and attachments, as well as build relationships between tables and navigate between screens. This chapter is intended to provide a glimpse into the capabilities of **Microsoft Dataverse** as a data platform, which will be useful in evaluating the upgrade options once your application starts to mature and needs more enterprise governance, capabilities, and capacity. Once you have developed a good understanding of Microsoft Dataverse architecture, we will look at the situations where you may want to consider upgrading from Microsoft Dataverse for Teams to Microsoft Dataverse.

In this chapter, we will learn about the following topics:

- Uncovering Microsoft Dataverse Layers
- Considering an upgrade from Dataverse for Teams to Dataverse

Let's start by removing the covers and peeking under the hood of Microsoft Dataverse and understand the different layers.

Uncovering Microsoft Dataverse Layers

Microsoft Dataverse is a data platform that allows you to store and model a variety of data and business logic to support interconnected applications and processes in a secure and compliant manner. As seen in the following diagram, Microsoft Dataverse consists of **Storage**, **Metadata**, **Compute**, **Security**, and **Lifecycle Management** components:

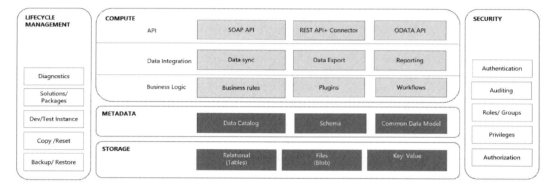

Figure 5.1 – Microsoft Dataverse composition

Let's take a quick look at each one of these components and their functionalities.

Storage Layer

The Storage layer consists of different types of storage solutions that cater to different needs and types of data. The types of data storage that are available are **Relational** data, **File** storage, and **Observational** data (also referred to as **Key: Value** or **Log** data).

Relational data

Relational data is stored in **tables** (also previously known as **entities**) with rows and columns. Relational data also helps you to build relationships between different tables.

At this juncture, we will take a slight detour to quickly look into **Entity Relationships**. We will also learn how data is stored in tables to get the optimum performance, scale, capacity, and throughput from the system.

A simple example here would be that of a set of students and educational courses that they would like to enroll in at a university. This can be modeled as follows:

- Student information (for example, **First name**, **Age**, and **Grade**) can be in a single table called **STUDENT**.

- Courses that this student is supposed to enroll for can be stored in a separate table called **COURSE** (including **Course ID**, the **Faculty** member who is going to teach this course, **Course Start Date**, **Course End Date**, **Credits**, and **Fees**).

- The mapping of courses that students enrolled in can be stored in a third table, which can be named **CLASS** (or **SESSION**), which will have the mapping of students and courses.

The **Entity-Relationship (ER)** diagram shows how this information can be represented graphically, as seen here:

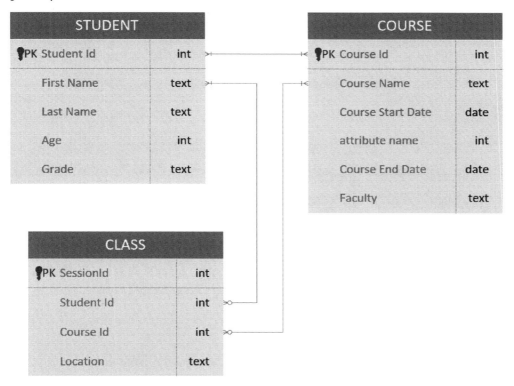

Figure 5.2 – Data modeling using the Entity-Relationship diagram

This is an example of a one-to-many relationship, which can be set up since one student can enroll in many courses. There can be several other entities in the system, such as **Faculty**, **Seat**, and **Registration**, and several relationships can be set up between these entities. For example, if we also include **Faculty** as a table, in order to extend the schema and add actors to the system shown in the preceding diagram, we can establish another relationship between **Faculty** and **Course** (that is, a course may be taught by one or more faculty members).

This process of defining tables (entities), their **columns** (also previously called **fields** or **attributes**), and their relationships, is called **Data Modeling**. During modeling, it is also recommended to optimize, reduce, or eliminate redundant columns being shared in tables. This optimization process (called **normalization**) is achieved by splitting the table (with redundant rows) into two or more tables. The simplest way to explain this would be to reference *Figure 5.2*. If **Faculty Name** and **Faculty ID** are added right inside the same **COURSE** table, it would be in a de-normalized state. A regular normalization process would be to split such a course table and create another faculty table with its own attribute (Faculty ID, Faculty Name, and other relevant attributes if needed) and then establish a relationship with the course table as explained earlier. In the example here, for a given faculty ID, the faculty name would always be the same. There is no reason why both the faculty ID and faculty name need to be duplicated in the course table for every record; a faculty ID is sufficient, and which can then be used to look up the rest of the information about the faculty from the **Faculty** table.

All such data modeling can be done inside Microsoft Dataverse, based on real-life entities or objects, and how they relate to each other within the system.

Many database developers are already aware of this ER concept and various types of relationships that can be set up (one-to-one, one-to-many, many-to-many, and a few other variations), along with the normalization that is part of data modeling.

For a citizen developer, the concepts of ER, data modeling, and normalization might look a little overwhelming to begin with. However, most citizen developers should be able to learn data modeling and normalization as they start deciding on the tables that map to their entities in the system. You will get better with these skills eventually as you try to design and build more real-world applications. The good news here is that normalization techniques are not always required and never ideally completed; you learn and tweak things as the application evolves. However, normalization sometimes causes performance issues since there are more tables to be queried and joined. In this case, performance experts would then denormalize and merge some tables to achieve better performance from the system.

The takeaway from this section is that, with Microsoft Dataverse, you can model your data and set up such relationships between your tables (entities).

File data

While storing data for any applications, there may come a scenario where there is a need to attach pictures, documents, or other **filetype** data to a transaction. For example, in the preceding scenario, where a student enrolls on a course and pays a fee, the receipt of this transaction could be generated and stored inside Microsoft Dataverse. Similarly, another scenario could be that of building a home/site inspection app, where the photographs of the home/site could be captured, stored as files, be related to each inspection record, and saved in the **Inspection** entity table. Since Microsoft Dataverse supports files as a native data type, the experience of building an app that needs a file data type becomes effortless.

Key: Value Data

There are several application scenarios where data is written once but read multiple times, such as single lookup values like the head of the department, indexes to file locations, or simply an activity logging such as `file<filename> <create/read/updated/ deleted> by <person> at <datetime>`. Such data, which falls into the category of NoSQL data, can also be stored in Microsoft Dataverse.

Using Microsoft Dataverse for IoT data

It is important to note that data from **IoT** (short for **Internet of Things**) devices, such as hourly temperature readings from a smart thermometer placed in all ovens of a bakery or the conference rooms of a business complex, qualifies as observational data and is usually in the format `<ScanDateTime> <Room#> <ObservedReading>`. However, IoT data can be voluminous and generated at a very high frequency and scale, depending on the devices sending these datasets, but it may just be raw data collected and not of much business value. Unless there is a dataset of business interests, in other words, an outlier observation (data that lies above or below a specific range) that deserves to be highlighted and action taken, it is recommended that in such cases, raw data is directed to other NoSQL data storage options such as Azure Cosmos DB (`https://azure.microsoft.com/en-gb/services/cosmos-db`) or Azure Data Lake Storage (`https://docs.microsoft.com/en-us/azure/storage/blobs/data-lake-storage-introduction`). The dataset that is of interest to the business can then be ingested into Microsoft Dataverse, at an interval that suits requirements, using Dataflows (`https://docs.microsoft.com/en-us/powerapps/maker/data-platform/create-and-use-dataflows`) or OData API connectors.

The interesting part about using Microsoft Dataverse for storing all these types of data is that the developer doesn't need to worry about implementing or architecting different storage solutions for different types of data. Microsoft Dataverse automatically handles the storage of different types of data based on the best storage solution and the same set of **APIs** (short for **Application Programming Interfaces**) for professional developers and connector operations (for citizen developers), regardless of how and where the data is stored by Microsoft Dataverse.

Now that we have looked at the storage layer, let's take a quick look at the metadata layer components.

Metadata Layer

Metadata, as the name states, is information about the primary data that is going to be stored inside Microsoft Dataverse. The data stored in Microsoft Dataverse is used in multiple places throughout the platform to render experiences such as form design, data grids, or even the API layer, which is used in building custom applications. The simplest example here would be that of a standard entity, **Account**, which is available out of the box inside Microsoft Dataverse.

While **Account** is a standard entity, represented as a table in Microsoft Dataverse, some of the attributes, such as **Display Name** and **Plural Name** of the entity, can be customized. For example, in the student enrolment example that we looked at earlier, instead of creating a new custom entity, we can use this standard entity named **Account**. The name "Account" refers, in general, to the primary player/actor within the system. In the business world, this is often referred to as **Customer Account** or **Account**. In the preceding example, such changes made to the entity/table definition would be stored in the metadata layer and made available to the other parts of the platform. Now that you understand what is often referred to as metadata, let's look at the other components in the Metadata layer – the Schema and Data catalog – in the following sections.

Schema

The blueprint or structural description of components such as tables, columns, and relationships between various tables in a database or data store is often referred to as the **Schema**. In Microsoft Dataverse, you can create new tables and extend existing tables to add custom columns. All these capabilities are facilitated by the Schema definition layer of Microsoft Dataverse.

Now that you understand the definition of a schema a bit better, let's look at how a common schema helps us to establish some industry-wide patterns using the common data model.

Common Data Model

The **Common Data Model** is a standard schema that consists of tables, columns (fields/attributes), and relationships that you would come across in any application. Just like the **Account** entity example, there are several such entities, including **Contact** and **Task**, that are included in the common data model. The biggest advantage of leveraging this schema is that Microsoft has poured its experience of building **Business Applications** products, over all these years, into building this common schema that you can leverage, and thereby save you a lot of time when doing data modeling and normalization. You get a big jump start as a citizen and professional developer by just having to focus on wiring the business logic and user experience. This common schema also plays a big role in building a shared understanding of the underlying schema across different groups within an organization. By doing so, it helps them to build customizable business applications, to serve the needs of their users, and, by extension, to meet the future needs of the organization.

More information about the different schemas in the common data model can be found here: `https://github.com/Microsoft/CDM`.

> **Important note**
>
> *What is the difference between the common data model (CDM) and Microsoft Dataverse?* The CDM is a model or definition, like a template, of how the most frequently used entities/tables, attributes/fields, and relationships can be designed. You can leverage this definition and build applications on any data platform, such as Azure SQL or **Amazon Relational Database Service** (**Amazon RDS**). However, Microsoft Dataverse is a data platform, as seen in the composition diagram (*Figure 5.1*) at the beginning of this chapter, that allows you to store and model a variety of business data and logic to support interconnected applications and processes in a secure and compliant manner. The CDM also helps industry domains (for instance, healthcare, finance, and manufacturing) to build a common schema that is uniform across the industry. For example, you can see the schema for healthcare through this link, `https://docs.microsoft.com/en-us/common-data-model/schema/core/industrycommon/healthcare/healthcare-overview`, and you will understand the utility of having a common data model for clinical, mediation, and other modules described in the model. It helps establish all medical software to build a common schema for billing, diagnostic reports, and so on.

Besides the CDM, Microsoft Dataverse also allows developers to define their custom schema and a catalog of other business data sources that can be integrated, such as SAP, SQL, DB2, or Oracle databases.

Data Catalog

Data catalog can be considered as an inventory of all the data contained inside Microsoft Dataverse. It is very much like an index of a book, which you can use to discover and retrieve the data that is needed. Both the schema and data catalog act as the glue between the compute and storage layers by abstracting much of the implementation details. For example, as a citizen developer or professional developer building an app in Microsoft Dataverse, you can query for all the entities (tables), their attributes (columns), and other information about the core data stored in Microsoft Dataverse. Thus, you can discover, observe, and navigate through different data elements, akin to browsing through a catalog.

To summarize this section, we have seen that the metadata layer of Microsoft Dataverse provides a lot of flexibility and modeling assistance to bring any kind of data to build your application.

We will look at the compute layer of Microsoft Dataverse in the next section.

Compute Layer

The compute layer is a combination of functionalities that fall into three broad categories – the **API**, **Data Integration**, and **Business Logic** sub-layers.

Business logic

As you start building business applications, you will come across business rules that are specific to a business, industry, organization, school, or even just a small team.

One example of business logic, in the case of the student-course scenario, could be that a student who is a resident of the local state is given a 20% discount from their enrollment fees. Another example could be that the organization has a policy of not conducting classes on the last Friday of the month, and in such cases, all classes scheduled for the last Friday of the month should get rescheduled either to the next Monday or the following Friday, as per the policies of the organization that is implementing them.

Such business logic needs to be applied across all the applications built within the organization, and hence it makes sense to apply this in one place, that is, the compute layer, rather than implementing it in every individual instance. This is an optimal way to design your system as there is only one place where such business logic will need changing, as part of changing business needs, rather than modifying all the applications that have been built. This business logic layer in Microsoft Dataverse has business rules, workflows, and plugins that we will learn more about in subsequent sections.

Business rules

Business rules allow you to configure rules on the data that would be added to the system. Please refer to the following screenshot for guidance on how you can set up business rules in Microsoft Dataverse without writing a single line of code:

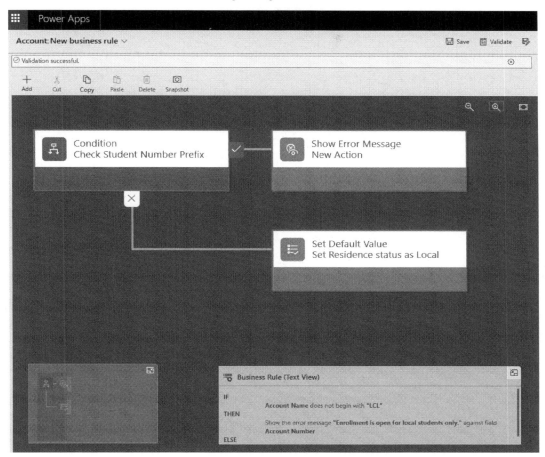

Figure 5.3 – Business rules designer in Microsoft Dataverse

For example, in the case of student enrolment, you can add a rule to ensure that the student number should start with LCL to qualify for enrolment. This can be easily achieved by using the business rules designer, which can be found in the **Business Rules** section for each entity/table within Microsoft Dataverse.

Workflows

Workflows are helpful in speeding up the predefined flow of business processes without any user interaction. Microsoft Dataverse provides two types – background workflows and real-time workflows. Both types of workflow accomplish nearly the same type of tasks, such as creating, deleting, and assigning a record. However, background workflows execute asynchronously when resources are available, while real-time workflows are executed instantaneously as soon as the conditions for triggering the workflow are met. Generally, background workflows are recommended as they help balance the resource consumption on the server and improve performance across the system for all users. Power Automate flows can also be used to achieve business process automation by leveraging the out-of-box connectors to Microsoft Dataverse.

A workflow usage scenario can be illustrated using the student enrolment example we discussed in the *Relational data* section earlier. For example, the student account can be updated to process a discount in enrolment fees, based on residency status, as shown in the following screenshot:

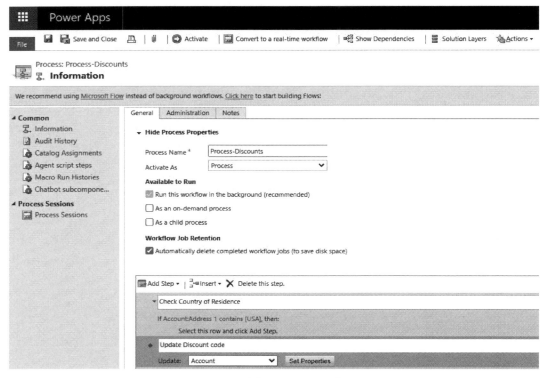

Figure 5.4 – A workflow in Microsoft Dataverse

As seen in the preceding screenshot, the workflow can be configured to run in real time or in the background by checking the **Run this workflow in the background (recommended)** option. While the scenario of processing a discount in enrollment fees might be needed in real time, in some scenarios, where invoices are generated at the end of the day or end of the month, this workflow can be marked to be run in the background.

> **Recommendation: Use Microsoft Power Automate Flow over workflows**
>
> Microsoft Power Automate is a recommended option that is now available on the Power Platform, which is an advanced and much better version of configuring automated workflows, as compared to the native legacy workflow inside Microsoft Dataverse.

Plugins

Plugins are often preferred by professional developers since they require you to write .NET code and the resulting assembly is registered to specific events within the event framework, which provides more flexibility to modify or augment the platform's behavior.

> **Important note**
>
> The most important difference between a plugin and a workflow is that a workflow is a more declarative way of configuring certain behavior, so it is limited by what is available in the designer, whereas a plugin allows professional developers to go beyond the limits of what is possible from the designer.

Most of the scenarios achieved through workflows can be achieved through plugins, but the same cannot be said for the reverse scenario. Plugins are more capable but do require professional development skills to build and register them within Microsoft Dataverse.

For the scope of this book, as we are focused on Citizen Developers, we will not delve much into the plugins, so let's look at the next category in the compute layer.

Data Integration

Microsoft Dataverse provides various ways to bring or generate data into the platform, as well as integrating existing data that might already be available in some other data sources. In this subsection, we will take a quick look at the options provided by Microsoft Dataverse – **Data Sync**, **Data Export**, and **Reporting**.

Data Sync

Data Sync is a feature in Microsoft Dataverse that helps in keeping the data within the common data system in sync with another parallel system that might be used for other purposes. For example, a task or appointment created in Outlook can be synchronized into Microsoft Dataverse so that you can see these tasks side by side when using an application built on Microsoft Dataverse. For example, in the scenario of student enrolment, a class schedule can be synchronized with the personal calendar of a faculty.

> **Important note**
> For more details on Integration with Office 365, you can refer to this blog: `https://powerapps.microsoft.com/en-us/blog/office-365-integration-features-in-common-data-service`.

Similarly, another powerful feature that falls into this area is the ability to handle mobile offline scenarios. The offline capability allows applications built on Microsoft Dataverse to go offline (for example, in airplane mode on mobile, or no data/internet connection areas) and continue working with offline cached data on the device, including making changes, which then get replayed and synchronized with the server when the connection is restored.

While it is understood from the preceding scenarios that there are cases where Microsoft Dataverse can help to keep the data in sync and updated, let's look at a scenario where the high business value data stored inside Microsoft Dataverse can also be exported to other systems.

Data Export

Some of the important capabilities to highlight here are the ability to export or replicate data out of Microsoft Dataverse and into Azure Data Lake and Azure SQL Database (which is hosted in your own subscription). As the organization grows, so does the need to do custom reporting and keep a close eye on the data and key performance indices.

Data Export Service (DES) is one such feature of Microsoft Dataverse that allows customers to move/replicate data across into a data warehouse that can then be used for reporting and analytics. DES requires you to interact with a REST-based API for two types of operations – metadata operations and profile operations. This requires a professional developer to interact with the definition to set this up. More details on metadata and profile operations can be found at this link: `https://docs.microsoft.com/en-us/powerapps/developer/common-data-service/data-export-service`.

However, exporting data to Azure Data Lake is more declarative and can be achieved through a simple click-through wizard by providing your Azure subscription details.

Reporting

Microsoft Dataverse provides a few options for reporting.

The one option that is natively present in the platform leverage is **SQL Server Reporting Service (SSRS)**. Folks who are familiar with SSRS will find that both ways of generating a report – **Report Authoring Extension** and **Report Wizard** – are commonly used by SQL reporting experts.

You can connect to Microsoft Dataverse from Power BI by using the built-in options under **Get Data** and then choosing the **Power Platform** section, where you will discover the option to connect to Microsoft Dataverse by simply providing the environment URL, which you can find on your **Power Platform Admin Center (PPAC)**, in other words, `https://admin.powerplatform.microsoft.com/`. Once you provide the environment URL, you will see the option to browse the tables within Microsoft Dataverse and build reports, just like building reports using SQL server, as demonstrated in the following screenshot:

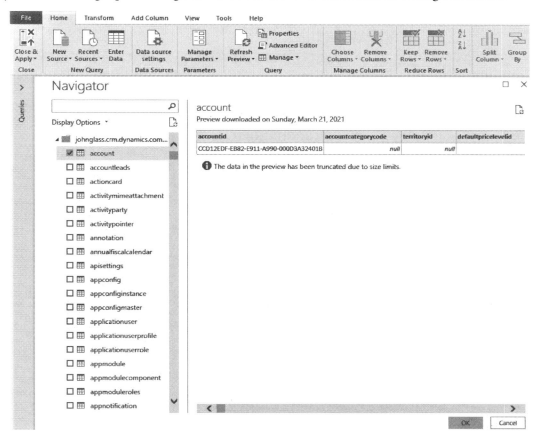

Figure 5.5 – Entity navigation in Power BI

The features and sections that we talked about in this *Compute layer* section of Microsoft Dataverse are just the major highlights or scenarios that are commonly used within Microsoft Dataverse. Several other features are present, with more being added as Microsoft Dataverse continues to become the center of data gravity for all business applications.

API (Application Programming Interface)

This layer of Microsoft Dataverse supplies the APIs that are useful for professional developers and other applications (Power Apps, Power BI, and so on) to connect to Microsoft Dataverse. The easiest way to explain this would be in the data integration scenario with Power BI. You will see that once you provide the Microsoft Dataverse instance URL as `https://yourenvironmentid.crm#.dynamics.com`, you can connect to the Microsoft Dataverse instance. This is because Power BI and other such applications can talk to Microsoft Dataverse through the API layer. You can validate this by simply logging in to the instance from your browser and navigating to the Microsoft Dataverse instance URL, `https://yourenvironmentid.crm#.dynamics.com/api/data/v9.1/` (note that the text **api/data/v9.1/** is added to the end of the URL).

Let's look at some of the protocols used in the Dataverse APIs (OData and SOAP) and connectors in the subsequent sections.

OData

The API used in the preceding example is called the Microsoft Dataverse **Web API**. This Web API implements the Open Data Protocol (OData) endpoint, which is an **ISO** (short for **International Organization for Standardization**) approved standard for building and consuming RESTful APIs. A RESTful API means an API that follows the **REST** (short for **Representational State Transfer**) architecture. This architecture greatly simplifies the interaction between systems through APIs by providing a set of universal (agnostic of platform/tech), uniform, and predefined stateless HTTP operations. This implementation vastly reduces the bandwidth and improves the interoperability of systems. It is used by most modern-day applications for implementation and discoverability as actions are performed based on transport protocols such as HTTP, GET, POST, PUT, and DELETE.

More details about this topic can be found at `https://www.odata.org/`.

SOAP

Microsoft Dataverse also supports another web service known as the Organization service. This Organization service is optimized for .NET Framework, which is not RESTful but based on **SOAP** (Simple Object Access Protocol). SOAP is an **XML**-based protocol for exchanging messages between interacting systems. It is more complex than OData in terms of implementation due to the additional layers of encryption and message definitions involved, besides conveying the contracts to interact with such services, often referred to as **Web Services Description Language** (**WDSL**).

REST API + Connector

Connectors (or **Data Connectors**) provide easy access to Microsoft Dataverse for citizen developers. REST APIs form the foundation of Microsoft Dataverse connectors, allowing citizen developers to not just connect to Microsoft Dataverse, but also to other data sources during the creation of low-code/no-code applications. Please see the *Understanding Data Connectors* section in *Chapter 2, Exploring Microsoft Dataverse for Teams*, to understand more about their role in low-code/no-code app development.

For the scope of this book, and the examples provided later in this book, we won't be interacting with these APIs much. Hence, the aim of this section on APIs was just to provide a glimpse into APIs and the capabilities available in Microsoft Dataverse that professional developers can explore.

So, let's now look at some of the other features, which are crucial for all modern-day organizations, usually referred to as Enterprise Platform Essentials – **Security** and **Lifecycle Management**.

Security in Microsoft Dataverse

The security features within Microsoft Dataverse are very expansive due to the options that support enterprise-grade security for your applications. For this book, we will only cover a subset of these features, including **Authorization**, **Privilege**, **Roles/Groups**, and **Auditing**, which will be relevant for building applications on Microsoft Dataverse. Let's start with the building blocks mentioned in the following sections.

Authorization

As a system of high-value business records, each data record and metadata contained inside the Microsoft Dataverse is of immense business value. So, all the records within Microsoft Dataverse are available only to an authorized user. The security model is constructed based on each artifact (components such as tables, columns, forms, and records) requiring appropriate privileges, that is, the ability to create, read, and update. With Microsoft Dataverse, this ability to control access to the data can be granted at Business Units, the Teams level based on business needs.

Privilege

Privilege is what determines the access level for each user to the data within Microsoft Dataverse. You can edit the access level for users by modifying their privileges within the system. The access level is a tier based on the hierarchy and ownership of the record that was created. These levels vary and could be granted at the individual user level or by being a member of a team, business unit, or at the organizational level. Standard privileges available in Microsoft Dataverse are **Create**, **Read**, **Write**, **Delete**, **Append**, **Append To**, **Assign**, and **Share**.

Roles/groups

The privileges mentioned in the previous section, when grouped together, are referred to as **Roles** or **Security Roles**. These roles can be associated with organizational roles and responsibilities performed. For example, somebody enrolling in a course would have the role of a student, while someone who needs to review and grade assignments will be assigned the role of faculty, and similarly, someone who has all the privileges in the environment would be assigned the role of system administrators. These roles can be assigned to users or also to security groups, also known as **Microsoft 365 groups**. Security groups help you to group together all users who need a similar set of privileges and thereby the same level of access. Administrators of the system are always advised to use a security group to control access to Microsoft Dataverse.

For example, a sales manager will have the privilege to convert a **lead** into **opportunity** or increase the discount value on the sales invoice. Actions such as this, converting a **lead** into **opportunity** and offering discounts, require privileges in the system. These privileges, as discussed, need to be granted on these **tables** (**lead**, **opportunity**, **Sales Invoice** available in Microsoft Dataverse) by a system admin. If there is a group of people with a similar privilege level (sales managers), then that forms the basis of creating a **role** in the system: **Sales manager**. Additionally, Microsoft Dataverse also provides the ability to set privileges for records at the global level or within their business units and teams. In bigger organizations, while assigning users and roles, it is too cumbersome for the security administrator to decide on privileges and roles to be granted to an individual. Microsoft Dataverse provides a default set of security roles, or you can create custom ones, such as "Global Sales managers," and assign them to individual users or groups from Azure Active Directory.

Authentication

Authentication is the process of validating the identity of the user or application that is trying to access the system containing resources or data, which is protected so as to be accessed securely. Microsoft Dataverse uses the **OAuth 2.0** protocol, which is an industry standard. For citizen development scenarios, the connector and API layers take care of the authentication and Citizen Developer doesn't need to know any of the details.

For professional developers who want to build standalone .NET client applications, you can find more information here: `https://docs.microsoft.com/en-us/powerapps/developer/common-data-service/authenticate-oauth`.

Auditing

Most organizations need to have access to the history of data interaction (such as system access by authorized and non-authorized individuals, especially in the event of a security breach). Using the auditing feature in Microsoft Dataverse, customers can enable auditing for entities, records, privileges, logs, user access, and so on. Auditing is configured at three levels – organization, entity, and attribute. Any user with a system administrator or system customizer role can configure auditing.

This concludes a roundup of the security features within Microsoft Dataverse. Now let's look at the life cycle management features of Microsoft Dataverse.

Lifecycle Management

Lifecycle management features that are worth highlighting for this book are the sandbox environment (also known as dev/test instances), **Solutions** and **Packages**, environment management operations (**copy**, **reset**, **backup**, and **restore**), and diagnostics.

As an application developer, one of the important things that you need to ensure is the quality of your application, especially not breaking an application that is live and being used by several users. There is a high likelihood of this happening while making changes to the applications, either to fix a bug or while introducing new features. To avoid such issues, you need to pay special attention to **Application Lifecycle Management (ALM)**. ALM is the process of managing different life cycle management phases, such as the development, maintenance, and decommissioning of a solution, product, or application being built. In the next section, let's look at how an application moves between different instances during ALM.

> **Important note**
>
> An environment is a collection or container of applications, flows, and an instance of Microsoft Dataverse.

Sandbox environment (dev/test instances)

While doing ALM, an application or product generally goes through broad phases of conceptualization, build, test, deploy, monitor, and fix. ALM needs to be followed through many iterative cycles, sometimes also referred to as the **DevOps** life cycle. While going through these phases, it becomes clear that there is a need to separate the production instance from the dev/test instance, so as to keep the application and data from getting corrupted. A typical application life cycle management looks like the flow diagram shown here:

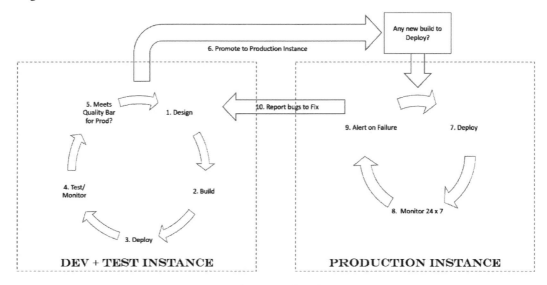

Figure 5.6 – Application Lifecycle Management

It starts with an ideation and design phase, followed by building, testing, deployment, and monitoring on the dev/test instance. For larger teams working on a common product or solution, this would be a daily affair where developers would check-in their changes, which would spin out a build/solution that would get deployed every day, followed by daily test suites being run, either manually or mostly through automated test suites. While these tests will try to simulate end user interactions, monitoring would detect failures and produce a stream of alerts/failures.

On analysis, this could turn out to be a real bug in the solution, which needs to be fixed, or it could be a bug in the testing code (code written to simulate usage). Depending on the severity of the impact and priority of the bug/issue, it may require a fix or rollback, of the solution deployed to production. In either case, this cycle repeats multiple times, until the solution meets the quality that is good enough for production deployment. Once the solution meets the bar, it will be queued for the next production deployment schedule.

Most production deployments need to be scheduled during off-peak hours, to avoid business disruption. Once deployed to production, similar monitoring efforts would be deployed to watch for failures in logs/telemetry due to customer interaction. This would be your signal to say that the recently deployed build broke some customer scenario(s). Once the logs are parsed and analyzed, you can decide to roll back the solution to the **LKG** (short for **last known good**) version or it can wait until the next solution version is available to be deployed, which could fix this issue. In either case, this bug that is reported needs to go back into the dev/test loop for consideration to be fixed in the next release to the production version. These iterations, which can continue until the application is sunset/decommissioned, are also referred to as **Continuous Integration and Continuous Delivery (CI/CD)**.

Each organization, depending on its level of maturity, adopts variations to this process to automate most of the elements involved in the CI/CD process, and what is depicted here is a generic example that can be followed as you begin this process. Some advanced automation here would be to set up a solution promotion to production to be automatically gated based on qualifying criteria, such as the percentage of failures and their types.

For professional developers interested in learning more about this, you can refer to `https://docs.microsoft.com/en-us/azure/devops-project/`.

A solution can be regarded as a vehicle to package and move changes between environments, analogous to a change build, and is explained in much more detail in the next topic of this chapter.

Solutions and Packages

All the application changes, along with metadata changes and customizations done to components of Microsoft Dataverse, are packaged into what are called solutions. You can compare this solution with an installable .msi, .app, or .exe file, or any application that you usually download from a public marketplace and install on your computer. Hence, as a citizen developer, once you create an application, with screens/forms and a schema (table definition for entities within Microsoft Dataverse), all these components should be made part of a solution so that all the relevant changes are packaged together and deployed for testing or production. Similarly, updates to the application will also be applied, either as a new solution or usually as a higher version of the same solution. So, solutions get applied on top of each other as layers and the last version wins in case of conflicts. Based on change management and the ALM perspective, solutions are also of two types:

- **Managed**: Managed solutions are certified builds (tested, verified, and sealed to prevent further changes). Managed solutions are used to deploy to any environment that isn't a development environment.

- **Unmanaged**: Unmanaged solutions can be compared to a non-certified build (live changes). Unmanaged solutions are therefore used in development instances while they are still under development or in the test phase. Unmanaged solutions can be exported either as unmanaged or managed.

While releasing solution files to a larger customer base as independent software, or publishing in a public marketplace as an **Independent Software Vendor** (**ISV**) solution, multiple such solution files can be bundled together with additional custom scripts, code, and configurations to ensure successful deployment in the customer's Microsoft Dataverse. Using the package deployer tool, you will be able to create such packages, also known as CRM packages. ISVs use one or more such packages to bundle their solution files, just like you would get a Windows application in a .exe or .msi format to be installed on a Windows OS (analogous to the Microsoft Dataverse platform in this scenario). You can get a good list of various ISV partners who are building solutions on Microsoft Dataverse platforms here: https://msdynamicsworld.com/power-platform/dataverse-cds.

> **Important Note**
> More details on how to create a package can be found here: https://docs.microsoft.com/en-us/power-platform/alm/package-deployer-tool.

Environment management operations

Microsoft Dataverse provides the functionality of maintaining different instances and taking backups of production instances to be used for test purposes besides allowing the resetting and copying of Microsoft Dataverse instances as needed. These environment management operations are explained here.

Copy

Using the copy feature, you can replicate or clone an instance of Dataverse. This is often used when you need to test different versions of solutions or upgrade scenarios. Similarly, this is also used to create a copy of the production environment to perform user acceptance testing as this would simulate the real production environment scenario. During copying, there is also an option to not copy the data but just the customization and schema, which is helpful in avoiding an increase in storage consumption on the platform.

Reset

Resetting an environment is very much like resetting a personal device back to factory settings. All the customization, apps, and data that were added to this environment are deleted and the environment is restored to the state it was at the time of creation.

Backup

Dataverse ensures that there is an automatic backup of the data every 10 to 15 minutes, known as system backups. Besides these automatic backups, you also have the option to create your own manual backup before carrying out major changes to the environment. These backups persist in the system for 7 to 28 days depending on the type of environment, be it production or sandbox.

Restore

As seen in the previous section, Dataverse allows you to create and maintain backups of the system snapshot at a point in time, which can be restored when required. While restoring environments, you have the choice to pick the specific backup and the target environment that the new restore environment would overwrite or replace. For safety reasons, this feature is only available for sandbox-type environments, and production environments can be restored only after an additional step of switching to sandbox environments before carrying out restore operations.

Diagnostics

Microsoft Dataverse is an extensible platform where users can add a lot of customizations, in the form of plugin code, workflows, custom forms, and controls. All these customizations can manifest themselves in either functionality problems or poor performance. To be able to troubleshoot this, Microsoft Dataverse provides diagnostics, such as a plugin trace log and workflow activity tracing, that can be enabled under administration settings. Additionally, there is an option to get more analytics and insights by configuring this diagnostics data into customers' own Azure Application Insights subscriptions. Such data, when available within customers' own Azure Application Insights subscriptions, helps customers to build their reporting to suit their organization's needs.

More details on this new feature are available here:

```
https://docs.microsoft.com/en-us/power-platform-release-
plan/2020wave2/power-platform-governance-administration/
microsoft-dataverse-errors-performance-data-diagnostics-data-
customers-own-azure-application-insights
```

Privacy and compliance

While privacy is not a layer or logical component that is called out, it is baked into these layers to ensure privacy is inbuilt through data protection at rest as well as in transit. In compliance with local regulations, you will also have data sovereignty since Dataverse ensures that customer data never leaves the geographical location in which the Dataverse instance is created. More information can be found here: `https://docs.microsoft.com/en-us/power-platform/admin/wp-compliance-data-privacy`.

To summarize, we looked at the different layers of Dataverse, including Storage, Metadata, and Compute. We also learned about the features in areas of security, privacy, and the administration perspective that help all enterprises to appreciate how Dataverse is a robust and secure data platform for building business applications.

Next, let's look at when we would need to upgrade from Dataverse for Teams to Dataverse

Considering an upgrade from Dataverse for Teams to Dataverse

Several factors will require you to upgrade your Dataverse for Teams environment to Dataverse, which we will cover in detail. The important considerations that would be involved in this decision are additional capabilities or capacity limitations, as outlined in the following sections.

Capabilities

Additional capabilities that would make you consider upgrading the environment into a Dataverse environment would be as follows:

- The ability to run the apps outside of Teams in a standalone browser, such as Google Chrome or Microsoft Edge, or as a native mobile app outside of Teams. Apps created within the Microsoft Teams environment would not be available anywhere outside of the Microsoft Teams application, such as a standalone browser or maker experience (`https://make.powerapps.com`). A maker experience is where you create standalone apps that can run on a browser or as a native mobile app.

- Any other direct API for integration purposes, such as adding data from a different data source to Microsoft Dataverse for Teams, wouldn't be allowed. Only a few approved scenarios can access Microsoft Dataverse through the API layer.

- The ability of the Team admin to manage the life cycle of the environment and manage the security permissions at a much more granular level.

Capacity

Since Microsoft Dataverse for Teams is available with your Office license at no extra cost, some capacity limitations apply here. These are as follows:

- The maximum amount of Dataverse for Teams instances that you can create under a tenant is restricted based on the number of eligible Microsoft 365 seats that provide the entitlement to use Microsoft Dataverse for Teams. It starts with an initial capacity limit of 5 environments to begin with for all customers, and an additional 1 environment per 20 Microsoft 365 seats is added to your quota.

- Each Dataverse for Teams environment has a 2 GB limit as regards data storage that includes relational data tables and file type attachments.

- The maximum amount of storage for the entire tenant allocated to Dataverse for Teams is also limited to 10 GB, plus an additional 2 GB per Dataverse for Teams environment (up to a maximum of 19.5 TB).

- Similarly, there are limits on the API calls for these Dataverse for Teams environments that are limited to 2,000 calls per user.

Since Microsoft can change the values, please refer to `https://docs.microsoft.com/en-us/power-platform/admin/about-teams-environment#capacity-limits` for the latest limits.

> **Licensing implications**
>
> Once the environment is upgraded to Microsoft Dataverse, then a premium Power Apps license is required to run these apps. Hence, there are some licensing implications in terms of upgrading Dataverse for Teams to a Dataverse environment, which we will cover in *Chapter 11, Licensing for Microsoft Dataverse and Dataverse for Teams.*

We will learn more about how the actual upgrade of a Dataverse for Teams environment is executed in *Chapter 9, Upgrading to Microsoft Dataverse Environment.*

Summary

In this chapter, you have developed a good understanding of Microsoft Dataverse and how Microsoft Dataverse is truly an enterprise-grade data platform that can be used to build enterprise-grade applications. Additionally, you have also seen the scenarios where you would consider upgrading your Microsoft Dataverse for Teams environment to a Microsoft Dataverse environment.

In the next chapter, we will look at adding Power Automate flows and Power Virtual Agents to augment the Health Scanner application.

6
Automating with Microsoft Dataverse for Teams

In the previous chapter, we took a detour on our app-building journey to take a deeper look into the capabilities of **Microsoft Dataverse** as a data platform. This will help you to have a broader understanding of the Power Platform capabilities and better design the architecture for enterprise-grade business solutions depending on the emerging business requirements of the organization.

In this chapter, we will learn how to automate business tasks using Power Automate flows in our Health Scanner application, by weaving in scenarios that you would encounter while building such applications. The goal is to demonstrate how the Power Apps application and Power Automate flows can combine organically to offer an integrated digital solution to your automation needs. Here are the topics we will cover in this chapter:

- Automating with Power Automate flows
- Building an automated flow
- Building an instant flow
- Building a scheduled flow

By the end of this chapter, you will be well versed in building different types of Power Automate flows and you will never want to waste your valuable time doing repeated tasks. Let's start by understanding what the different types of Power Automate flows are and how they could be useful in scenarios like the Health Scanner app.

Automating with Power Automate flows

In this section, we will look at how to create and invoke different types of Power Automate flows from within or outside the Health Scanner application. Such flows can be used to wire up any action as per the business needs, for example, sending a notification email.

Let's start by looking at the different types of flows that you can build and the different scenarios in which you will use them:

1. **Automated flows** are invoked automatically by the system based on the occurrence of an event that you select. These events could be the arrival of an email, the submission of a survey response, a case being resolved, or the creation of a new record in a Dataverse table or SharePoint list, and so on.

2. **Instant flows** are flows that can be triggered when needed through manual interactions such as the click of a button on a screen within an app or an action within Teams. You have seen how to add a button on a screen while building the Health Scanner application, and such buttons can be used to invoke an instant flow. Similarly, within teams, you have an option to extend message **Actions** to invoke a flow. Actions can be invoked by right-clicking a message posted in a teams' channel, as seen in the following screenshot:

Figure 6.1 – Actions in Microsoft Teams

There are out-of-the-box actions, and you can extend them by adding more custom actions with messaging extensions. Professional developers can extend these custom actions to invoke external web services using messaging extensions as outlined at this link: `https://docs.microsoft.com/en-us/microsoftteams/platform/messaging-extensions/what-are-messaging-extensions`.

For the context of this book and low-code/no-code extensions, this custom action can be thought of as invoking an instance flow.

3. **Scheduled flows** A **scheduled flow** is one where you can configure the flow to be initiated on a preconfigured schedule of your choice. Examples of such flows could be to send a daily summary report at the end of the business day, an appointment summary sent at 8 a.m. daily as a reminder of important events planned for the day, or to generate a monthly report and notify executives or management.

In the following sections, we will look at each of these different types of flows and build one of each type to integrate into the Health Scanner app and surrounding scenarios.

Building an Automated flow

In our scenario for the Health Scanner app, the manager of an employee who is scanned as having a body temperature greater than 99°F would need to be notified. In this scenario, when the notification is sent through an email, the manager can plan to carry out the mitigation plan as per the rules laid down within the organization.

For instance, the manager can plan for a substitute for this employee, approve sick leave, or arrange to move this employee to quarantine or provide them with a medical facility. In the following steps, we will see how this notification sending process can be automated, as soon as we have a scan record that meets the criteria, that is, a temperature reading of more than 99°F, without any manual intervention:

1. Click the **Automated** flow option from the **Build** hub, as shown in the following screenshot:

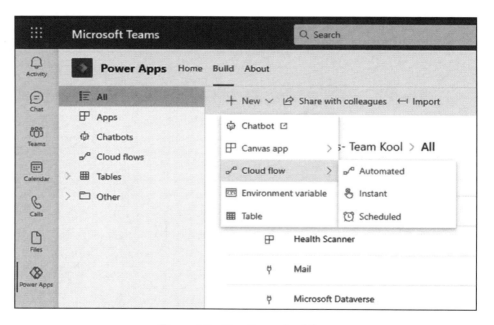

Figure 6.2 – Creating a cloud flow

2. On the next screen that comes up, you will see the option to configure a name and trigger for your flow, as seen in the following screenshot:

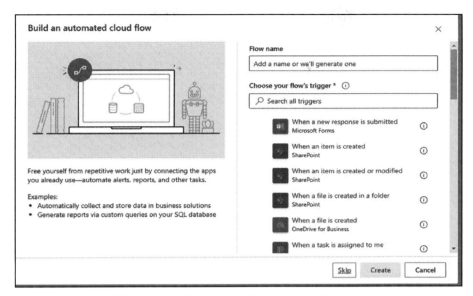

Figure 6.3 – Configuring the trigger for the flow

3. In the **Choose your flow's trigger** search box, type in `Dataverse` to filter out the trigger that we are going to use here – **When a row is added, modified, or deleted**. Provide the name `Inform Manager`, then select the **Dataverse** trigger and click **Create** to move forward:

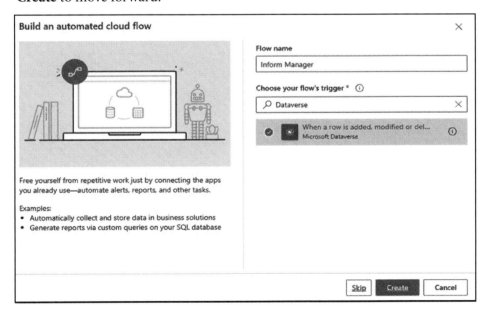

Figure 6.4 – Selecting the trigger

4. After you click **Create**, you will be presented with the option to choose the **Change type**.

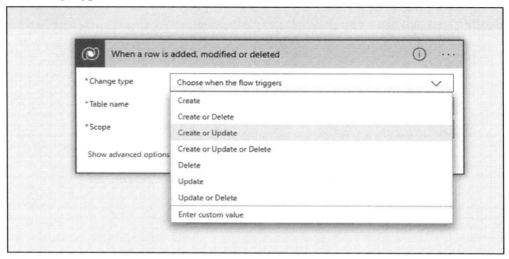

Figure 6.5 – Selecting the change type

5. Select the **Create or Update** option, so the notification gets sent out when creating or updating the body temperature in the app.

6. For the table name, choose the **Scan Detailses** table, which is where we stored all the scan records of employees, and for **Scope**, we will choose **Organization**:

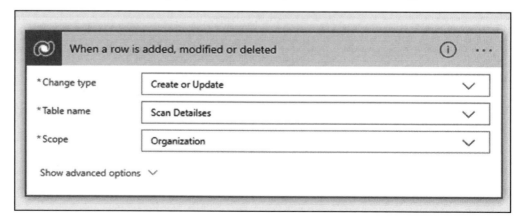

Figure 6.6 – Selecting the table and scope

There are other advanced options where you can provide an OData-style filter expression that will trigger this flow. For example, in our case, we can use **Row filter** to filter our scan records where the scanned body temperature is greater than 99. It is represented in an OData expression as crfc2_bodytemperature gt 99, where **crfc2_bodytemperature** is the **Name** of the column for body temperature in the Scan Detailses table and **gt** is the standard OData filter operator. You can find the list of other standard filter operators supported by Dataverse at this link: https://docs.microsoft.com/en-us/powerapps/developer/data-platform/webapi/query-data-web-api#standard-filter-operators

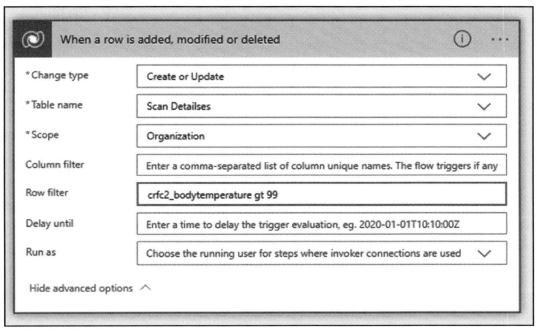

Figure 6.7 – Add Row filter to action

Another, simpler way to avoid using the OData expression is to leave the advanced options blank and instead use the Power Automate condition step, as shown in the following screenshot:

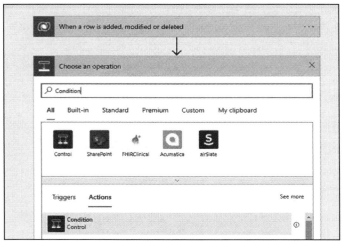

Figure 6.8 – Add a condition filter in a flow

As seen in the following screenshots (*Figure 6.9* and *Figure 6.10*), you will see that as soon as you select the condition, the flow branches out into the two alternatives, **If yes** and **If no**, which helps you to configure different actions based on the filter results.

7. To set the condition, click on **Choose a value** or **Add dynamic content**, which will bring up the option to choose the output values from the previous step in the flow:

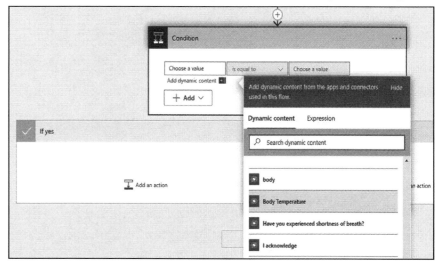

Figure 6.9 – Setting conditions in a flow

Here you can choose **Body Temperature** and change the condition to check if the value is greater than 99, as you can see in the following screenshot. When we compare values, there is no need to put additional quotes (either single or double) around the text or value. Every character put in this box will be used for comparison.

8. Next, in the **If yes** branch of the flow, choose the **Send an email(V2)** action from the **Standard Office 365 Outlook** connector.

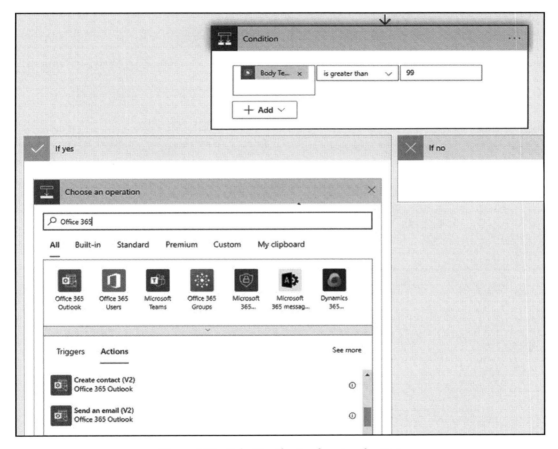

Figure 6.10 – Selecting the Send an email action

You can choose different means of notification actions provided by Power Automate, such as posting a message to a Teams channel or posting a message on Yammer, or several other options that are available out of the box. There is one step needed before we can send the email, which is to get the email and other details of the manager for the employee who needs attention.

9. Choose the **Get manager (V2)** action from the Office 365 connector, as shown in the following screenshot:

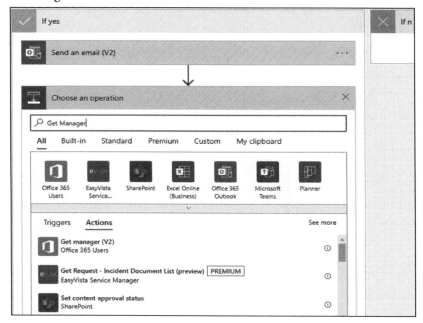

Figure 6.11 – Selecting the Get manager action

10. Once **Get manager (V2)** is selected, provide the email of the employee, which is available from the output of the previous step:

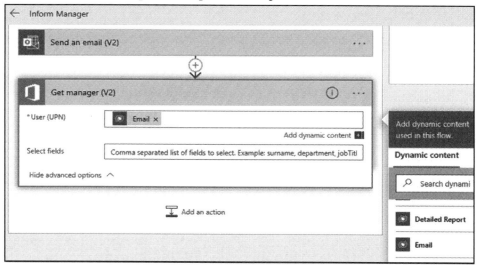

Figure 6.12 – Get manager details

11. Next, drag and drop the **Send an email (V2)** step below the **Get manager (V2)** step. This should now enable you to use all the manager details available from **Get manager (V2)** in your notification email, as seen in the following screenshot:

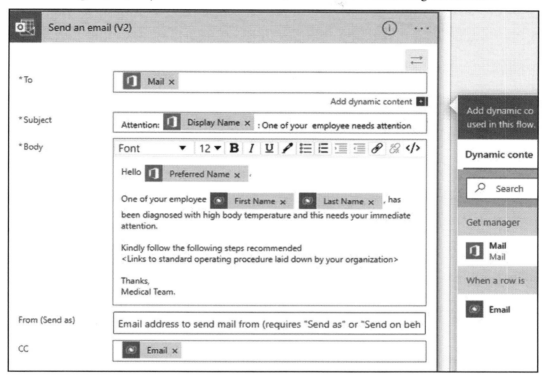

Figure 6.13 – Sending an automated email with dynamic values

You can observe that the **To** address is populated with the email address from **Get manager (V2)** to send the email to the manager. And the different dynamic values are used to show how these automated emails can be made personal and relatable by providing dynamic details such as addressing the manager with **Display Name** or **Preferred Name**. You can also see that **First Name** and **Last Name** of the employee can be provided. Additionally, as shown in the preceding screenshot, the employee can also be copied into such emails, if needed.

You can leverage the **Link** icon in the options available under **Body** to insert a link to internal resources. Additionally, you can use the **mailto:** tag in the closing signature line for the Medical Team in the email shown in the preceding screenshot.

12. Clicking on the **Link** icon will open a control with two values expected – **Link Title** and **Link Target**. As shown in the following screenshot, for **Link Title**, you will input display text such as `Click here` and for **Link Target**, you will provide the site URL. Similarly, in the case of the email address, you will provide `Medical Team` for **Link Title** and **Link Target** can be set to `mailto: MedicalTeam@ imaginaryelectronics.com`:

Figure 6.14 – Adding hyperlinks and mailto links within an email body

13. Once the flow is saved, use the flow checker on the right side of the editor to check for any errors before testing this flow.

To test this flow, all you need to do is to add a new record or edit the temperature reading of any previous record from the Health Scanner app. Once the record is created or updated to show a temperature reading of 99.1 or higher, you will see that the flow gets triggered, ideally within a few seconds.

Let's go to the app and add a new scan record or update the **Body Temperature** value to 99.5 for one of the employees, as shown in the following screenshot:

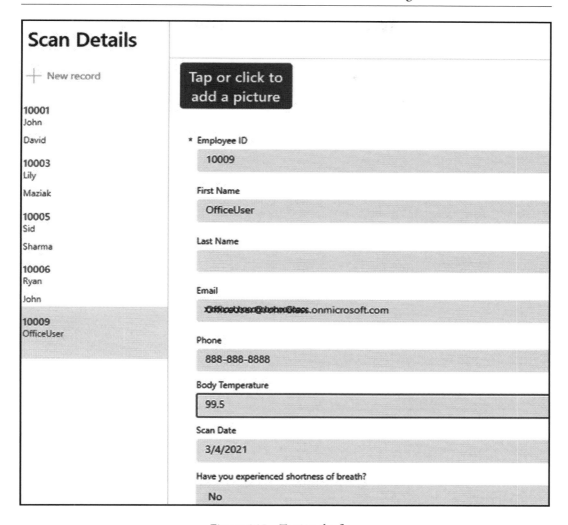

Figure 6.15 – Testing the flow

Once this record is saved, you will see that the manager and the employee with the email addresses in the record receive an automated email. The email address in the preceding screenshot is intentionally masked; it can be any valid email address of the employee within the organization.

14. Now navigate to **Build | See all | Cloud flows | Inform Manager** and click **Flow** to see various details, as shown in the following screenshot:

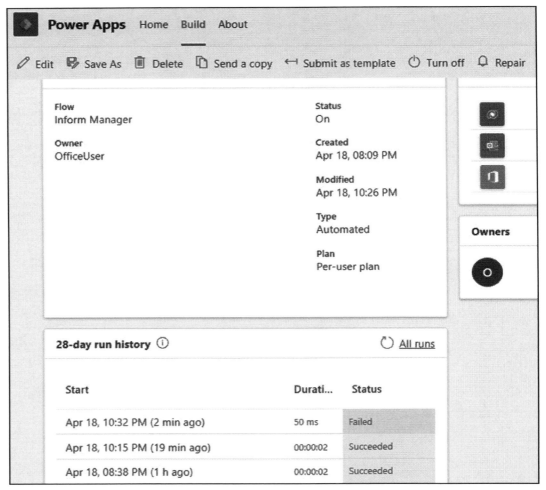

Figure 6.16 – Flow details

You can view the history of all runs (executions) and you can see their statuses as well. One of the recent runs failed due to an error that I intentionally inserted to demonstrate how you can troubleshoot and fix these issues from here.

15. To investigate the failure, just click on the failed instance and you will see the error details, as shown in the following screenshot:

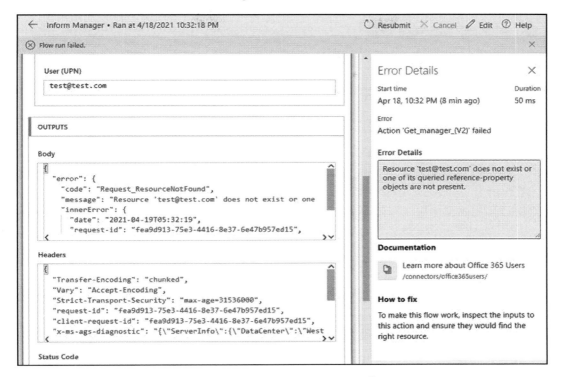

Figure 6.17 – Investigating errors in a flow

As you can see from the preceding screenshot, the wrong email address was provided for the employee – intentionally, just for the sake of this illustration – to get manager information, and hence the step to fetch the manager details of a non-existent employee failed.

16. If the employee's manager information was not configured while setting up the user's mailbox, then the flow would fail. To configure the user's manager, use the **Microsoft 365 admin center** as illustrated in the screenshot:

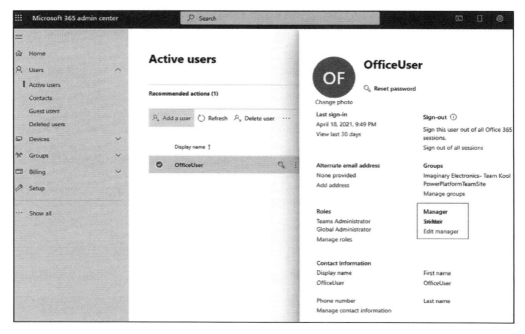

Figure 6.18 – Editing the user's manager information

You can also follow the details provided at the following link to configure manager information and other user details: `https://docs.microsoft.com/en-us/exchange/recipients-in-exchange-online/manage-user-mailboxes/manage-user-mailboxes?redirectedfrom=MSDN#bkwk_UsetheShelltochange`.

In this section, we have seen how an automated flow can be created to send a notification based on a trigger – when a new scan is recorded where the body temperature is reported to be above 99°F or an existing record is updated to a value of more than 99°F. This included learning about the following:

- Different types of triggers
- Adding conditions and branching the flow
- Using Office 365 connectors to get user properties
- Sending customized messages with dynamic values

In the next section, we will see how an instant flow can be invoked manually to perform the same action from a screen inside the Health Scanner app.

Building an Instant Flow

In this section, let's build an instant flow and then invoke it from one of the screens in the Health Scanner app. Instant flows are useful when human judgment is required before taking certain actions instead of just triggering a flow, as in the case of an automated flow, based on certain conditions being met. Let's start by creating an **Instant flow** from the **Build** hub, just like you initiated creating automated flows:

1. Click on the **New** button with the drop-down control, followed by **Instant** flow from the **Build** hub (as we did when we started creating an automated flow). On the new instant flow initiation screen, you will see the option to name the flow and select **Power Apps** as the source of the trigger, as shown in the following screenshot:

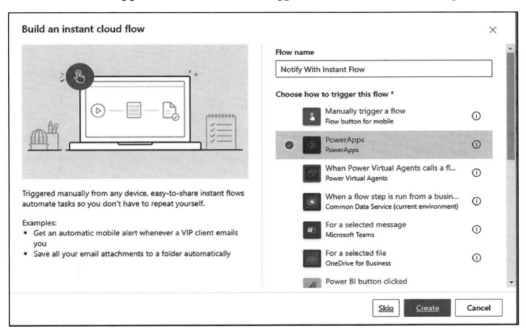

Figure 6.19 – Creating an instant flow

2. Let's name the flow `Notify With Instant Flow` and click **Create**. You will see the same Power Automate flow editor screen with the only difference here being that a Power Apps initial step is pre-created for you.

The steps after these are like what you did with the automated flow. The email address of the employee whose manager needs to be notified is obtained from the pre-configured Power Apps step at the beginning of the flow, as shown in the following screenshot:

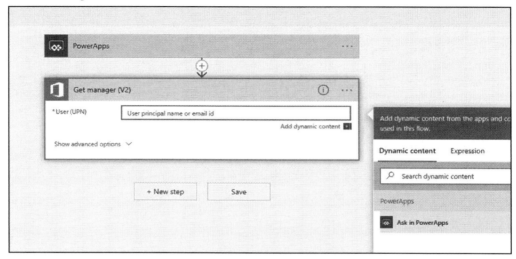

Figure 6.20 – Asking parameters from Power Apps

3. Clicking on **Ask in PowerApps**, as seen in the preceding screenshot, helps you to grab the email of the employee, provided from within the app. This email of the employee gets passed on to the next step in the flow, **Get manager (V2)**:

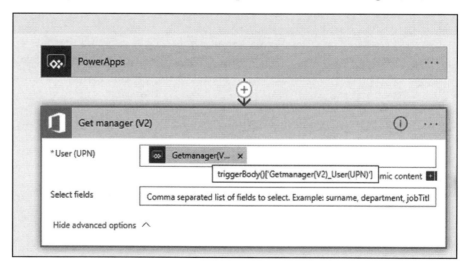

Figure 6.21 – Using values from a Power Apps based trigger

4. The next step is to add the notification email, just like we did in the automated flow in the previous section. As seen in the following screenshot, you will observe that we are limited to using just the email address provided by Power Apps in the **CC** field and within the email body, as compared to dynamic values such as first name, last name, and other information that was available in the case of the automated flow that we built in the earlier section.

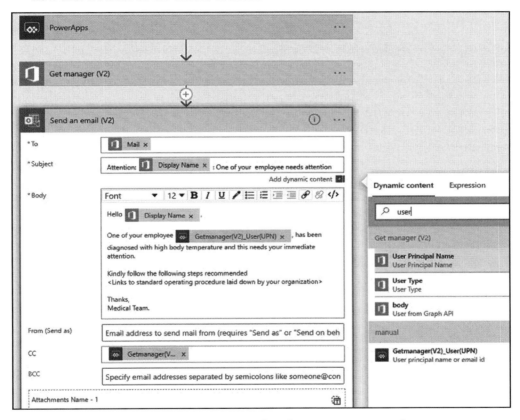

Figure 6.22 – Using dynamic values from Power Apps in a flow

All such information about the employee in the case of the automated flow was available from the previous step, that is, a trigger for the flow that was based on the row being created or updated in Dataverse.

5. The instant flow is now ready and can be tested from within the editor. Click the **Test Flow** icon in the top-right corner.

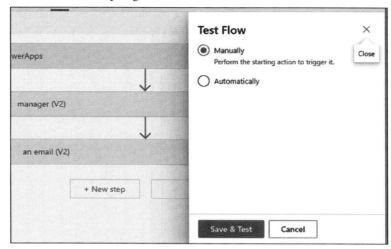

Figure 6.23 – Testing an instant flow

6. Chose the starting option as **Manually**, and proceed by clicking **Save & Test**. This will bring up the screen where you will be prompted to input the email ID or **UPN**. UPN refers to the **User Principal Name** attribute of Active Directory and is an internet-style login name with an @ symbol. By convention, this UPN usually maps to the email address of the user. These are required to trigger this instant flow, as seen in the following screenshot.

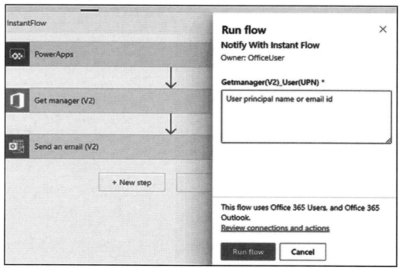

Figure 6.24 – Providing a parameter(s) for testing

This action is just simulating the actual scenario when the flow will be invoked with the click of a button on the app and the employee's email will be passed as a parameter to this flow.

7. Click the **Run flow** button after providing the email address of any employee, whose manager's details are also configured in the system.

8. Once the flow is tested successfully, you will see that the manager and the employee receive the notification email.

9. The next step is to add the button on the screen from where this flow can be invoked. Open the **NeedsAttention** screen of the Health Scanner application that we built in the previous chapters and add a button with the text **Notify**, as shown in the following screenshot:

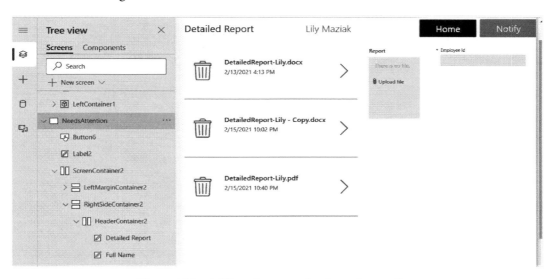

Figure 6.25 – Adding a button to invoke an instant flow

10. Next, click the three vertical dots on the menu options and then click **Power Automate** to bring up the pane on the right side of the screen that shows all the associated Power Automate flows. Please ensure that the **Notify** button was clicked before you do this to ensure that the flow is added to the control. You can confirm this from the title, which mentions the flows associated with the button; this is **Button6** in the following screenshot:

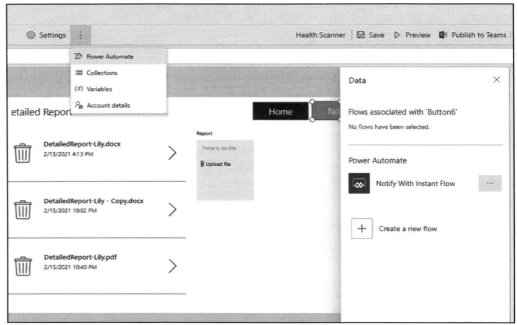

Figure 6.26 – Flow available to be invoked

If there is more than one instant flow created, then you will see all the flows listed under the **Power Automate** label seen in the preceding screenshot. Click the instant flow that you created in the previous step. This will result in the flow getting associated with **Button6**, as seen in the preceding screenshot.

11. Click on the flow to bind/associate with the button and, next, you will be prompted to set the **OnSelect** behavior of the **Notify** button to run this flow. As seen in the following screenshot, you can provide this function to invoke the flow – `NotifyWithInstantFlow.Run(NeedAttention.Selected.Email):`

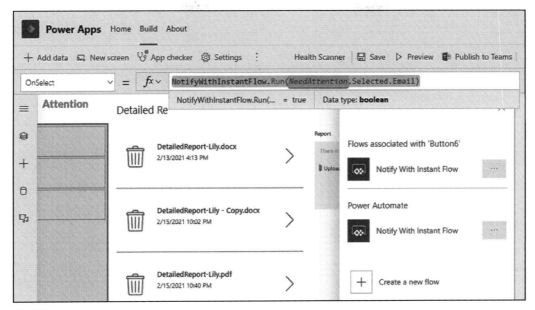

Figure 6.27 – Invoking the flow using the OnSelect behavior of the button

The `NeedAttention.Selected.Email` portion of the value ensures that the email of the employee whose details are being viewed on the screen is passed as a parameter to invoke the flow.

12. Save the app and you are now ready to test this instant flow invocation directly from the app. Launch the app in preview mode and then navigate to a few different employee records and click the **Notify** button to test the flow being invoked and emails being received by their managers. You can publish this version after testing is completed.

You have now learned how to build an instant flow and invoke this flow from a button in the Health Scanner app. Here is a quick recap of some of the topics that you learned about in this section:

- Creating a manual trigger such as a button in Power Apps
- Wiring up the button to invoke the instant flow
- Passing a value from the Power Apps to the instant flow

In the next section, let's see how to build a scheduled flow, which is another type of flow that can be scheduled to run at a pre-defined date and time.

Building a Scheduled Flow

In this section, we will see how we can use a scheduled flow to generate a daily summary report of all the employees, depending on the date of scanning. In the following steps, you can follow the instructions on how to get a scheduled flow created:

1. Click on **Build | New | Cloud flow | Scheduled** flow to start creating a scheduled flow. This brings up a screen like the one shown in the following screenshot:

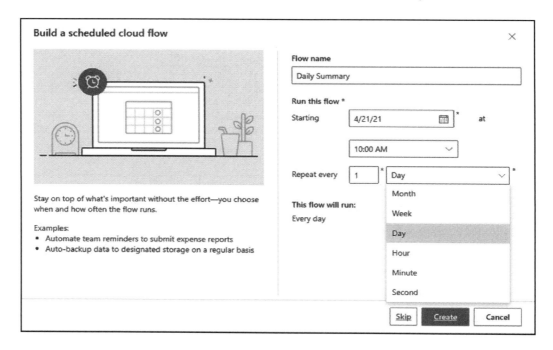

Figure 6.28 – Creating a scheduled flow

As shown in the preceding screenshot, you have a few options such as setting the start date, time, and frequency of execution. For this example, we will set it to run every day and then click **Create**. This will open the editor experience that we saw in the previous two types of flows.

2. Choose options such as setting the **Time zone** and deciding on the hours and minutes at which the flow can be scheduled throughout the day. Select the appropriate values based on your needs:

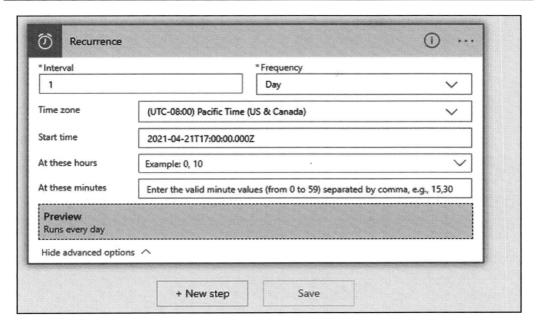

Figure 6.29 – Setting a schedule for a flow

3. After this, add a step to retrieve the list of employees who have been scanned since yesterday and were found to meet the criteria (a body temperature greater than 99). To do this, we will use the **Microsoft Dataverse** connector and leverage the **List rows** action, as seen in the following screenshot:

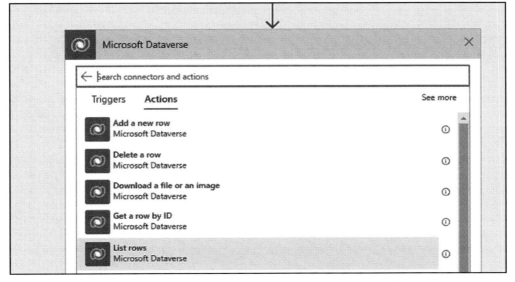

Figure 6.30 – Using a Microsoft Dataverse connector in a flow

As seen in the case of the automated flow that we learned about earlier in the chapter, there are other advanced options where you can provide OData-style filter expressions to filter the records or output.

4. Then add a row filter by using the OData expression `crfc2_bodytemperature gt 99`, where `crfc2_bodytemperature` is the name of the column for body temperature in the **Scan Details** table and `gt` is the standard OData filter operator.

    This is to filter the scan records where the body temperature scanned is greater than 99⁰F. Once we have the list of rows from Dataverse, based on the filter applied, we will add the next step to post a message to the Teams channel. Since we have already seen examples of using emails as a notification mechanism in previous types of flows, let's use the Teams channel here to illustrate the various options that you have. Based on your requirements, you can continue to use email or use any other means of notification, such as LinkedIn, Yammer, and so on, which are available as connectors to use.

5. For this scenario, add a **Post a message (V3)** action, available on the Microsoft Teams connector:

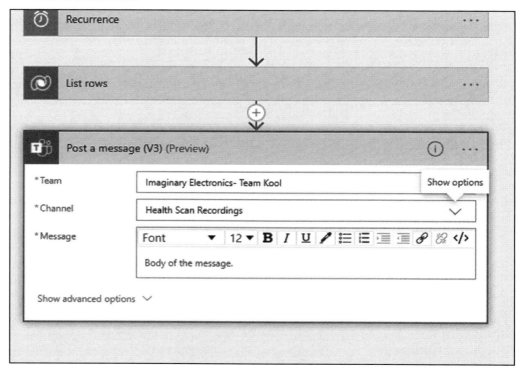

Figure 6.31 – Posting a message to a Teams channel from a flow

As soon as you add this next step of posting a message to a Teams channel, Power Automate flow will automatically create an **Apply to each** step. This is because the platform understands that whenever you use the **List rows** action, the output could contain more than one record and you would want to carry out all subsequent steps for each of the records returned.

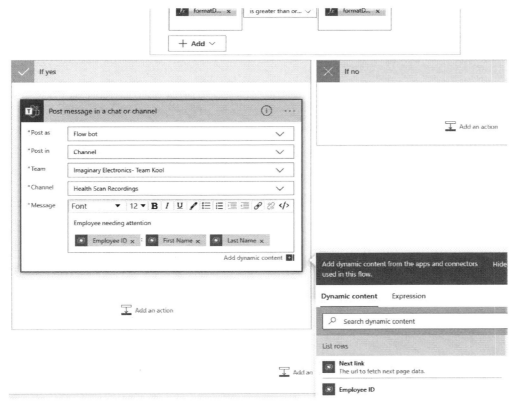

Figure 6.32 – Apply actions to each record within a flow

Within the **Post message in a chat or channel** action, choose the **Team** and **Channel** where you wish to post the message. Also add dynamic content such as **Employee ID**, **First Name**, **Last Name**, or any other column values desired, within the records returned from the previous step – **List rows** into the **Message**. You must have observed that we are getting all the records of employees scanned to date with a body temperature greater than 99⁰F. However, the goal was to provide a daily update or summary. It means that there is a need to filter the scanning period to just last one day so that we get to see incremental data on new scannings done since the previous day. For this step, we need to compare the date of scanning with the duration since the previous day and filter out other records.

6. Next, add a **Condition** step in a flow to compare these values, as shown in the following screenshot:

Figure 6.33 – Using expressions and conditions in a flow

Using the **Expression** options under **Add dynamic content**, you can add the following formulas to grab the scan date and interval (today -1) to filter out the results:

- `@formatDateTime(items('Apply_to_each')?['crfc2_scandate'],'YYYY-MM-dd'):`

This first expression, on the right side in the preceding screenshot, selects the `crfc2_scandate` value from among all the column values within the row, by passing the name of the column as defined in the table when we created it (refer to the table definition in the Build hub to get the exact name of the column here). The item `('Apply_to_each')?` is used to refer to the collection of rows, and finally, the `formatDateTime()` function is applied to get the output in a common data format, YYYY-MM-dd. This format helps us to have a common format when comparing with the next expression, on the right side in the preceding screenshot, which represents today's date -1 day (in the past).

- `@formatDateTime(addDays(utcNow(),-1),'YYYY-MM-dd'):`

  The `addDays()` function is used to add/subtract days. It's used to reduce the date by one day before comparison.

7. Your scheduled flow is now ready to test. Just click the test button in the top-right corner of the screen and run the flow. Please ensure that your Scan Detailses table does have records that meet the criteria, that is, a body temperature greater than 99 and a scan date that reflects today's date.

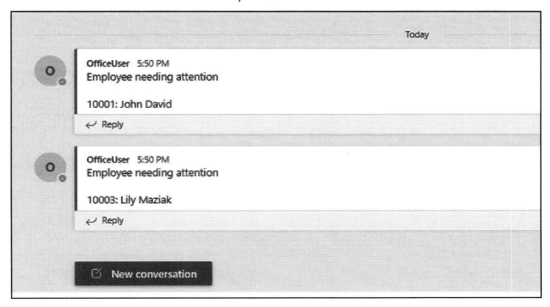

Figure 6.34 – Message posted from a flow

We have seen how you can use different types of Power Automate flows to automate business operations that make digital transformation a reality, without much or any coding at all.

Summary

In this chapter, we have seen different types of Power Automate flows – automated, instant, and scheduled flows– and the different scenarios where these could be used. We also covered some of the concepts that are often needed for building flows, such as different types of triggers – including the ones based on Dataverse, filtering datasets based on OData expressions, conditions for branching the flow of automation, adding dynamic content in flow actions such as sending messages via Teams or email, expressions to compare data, different types of connectors (Dataverse, Office 365, Teams), and corresponding actions supported by these connectors. Finally, we also saw how to test and troubleshoot common issues that you come across while creating a flow. The illustrations in this chapter do not cover the whole breadth of features and it is highly recommended that you play with additional scenarios and learn to incorporate them based on your needs.

> **Power Automate flows outside Dataverse for Teams**
>
> The concepts and Power Automate features that you learned about in this chapter apply to standalone Power Automate flows as well, which you can try at `https://preview.flow.microsoft.com/`. These standalone Power Automate flows don't need to use Microsoft Teams and can be built independently and used across the organization. You also get to use a larger set of premium connectors that are not available in the Teams version. However, end users of such flows are required to have a premium Power Apps or Power Automate license to be able to use them as standalone flows. We will cover the details of the licensing aspect in *Chapter 11, Licensing for Microsoft Dataverse and Dataverse for Teams*.

In the next chapter, we will learn about Power Virtual Agents and how to build a chatbot for the Health Scanner scenario that we have been using so far. We will also look at how the Power Automate flows that we built in this chapter can be reused within the Power Virtual Agents bots. This is often how enterprise applications are built and maintained, that is, building re-usable artifacts such as flows or libraries of code and reusable functions, and then using them as LEGO® blocks to put together business-critical solutions.

7

Building Power Virtual Agents Bots with Microsoft Dataverse for Teams

In the previous chapter, we looked at how Power Automate flows can help you to automate a lot of business tasks without writing a single line of code. In this chapter, we will leverage the power of **Power Virtual Agents** (**PVA**) in the Health Scanner application, by authoring a chatbot that will help answer the end user's questions. This bot will then be augmented with the Power Automate flows that we built in the last chapter, to automate business processes or tasks.

Here are the topics we will cover in this chapter, while learning how to build a Power Virtual Agent bot:

- Understanding Power Virtual Agent bots
- Creating a Topic for the Power Virtual Agent bot
- Adding flows to the Power Virtual Agent bot
- Publishing the Power Virtual AgentPVA bot

By the end of this chapter, you will have learned how to create a Power Virtual Agent bot, how to add different topics that the chatbot can converse with, how to invoke preconfigured actions through Power Automate flows from within a bot, and then finally, publishing the bot to a team or the entire organization.

Let's start with understanding what a Power Virtual Agent bot is, the different types of bots, and how they could be useful in scenarios, such as the Health Scanner app.

Understanding Power Virtual Agent bots

In this section, we will start with getting a basic understanding of a bot and the different types of bots that you will come across, before jumping into building a Power Virtual Agent chatbot. This chatbot can be integrated into your Teams experience and help answer questions about the Health Scanner app and the scenarios surrounding it.

A **bot** (derived from **robot**) usually refers to any autonomous program that runs based on software code written by a developer and often needs a trigger (the clicking of a link or a button, surfing a website, or even a preconfigured date and time becoming current) to be executed. A bot, just like a robot, can be used to do mundane tasks that humans get bored doing repeatedly. However, since these bots could trigger tasks that can run in the background (without any visual interface for the user), they are often misused by hackers, with malicious intent, to steal personal data or credentials when the user clicks a link or surfs a website, either knowingly or unknowingly.

A chatbot is a type of bot that is created to engage with users and communicate with them through messaging channels such as text messages or social media posts. Such chatbots are commonly used in customer service and are often seen on websites either to provide additional information or guide you with a support request or complaints. Within an organization, such chatbots are often used for different functions, such as by the IT department to address the most frequently asked questions or tasks such as resetting passwords, providing the location to download specific software, or logging a service request.

Now that you understand what a bot is and how chatbots could be used, we will see how PVA can help you to create a chatbot without writing a single line of code. This PVA chatbot can be integrated into a Teams channel and can help answer **frequently asked questions**, commonly referred to as **FAQs**, and take automated action. The FAQs could include inquiring about business hours for an organization, or in the case of the Health Scanner app, it could be used to find out which employee needs attention today. Automated actions could be something such as informing the manager of an employee that needs attention or alerting the medical team to attend to an employee who is sick.

To start with any Power Virtual Agent chatbot, we need to first start with the building blocks of a chatbot, which are called **Topics**. In the next section, we will start by creating the topic that we will be focusing on in our scenario.

Creating a Topic for Power Virtual Agent bot

Once topics are created, these topics come together to provide an integral chatbot experience. In this section, we will be authoring a topic that can carry out a couple of tasks, such as seeking information for a daily summary on health scans or informing the manager of a particular employee.

The following steps will help you to add PVA to your team before beginning with topic authoring:

1. Click on the three horizontal dots (**...**) on the Microsoft Teams rail and search for `Power Virtual Agents`. Using the **Pin** option, attach the **Power Virtual Agents** option to the Teams rail to the left of your screen, as shown in the following screenshot:

Figure 7.1 – Pinning Power Virtual Agents to Teams

Once this is done, you will land on the **Home** page, where you can quickly get started with creating a new bot.

2. However, another option is to use the **Chatbots** menu option and use the **New chatbot** option to create a new chatbot, as illustrated in the following screenshot:

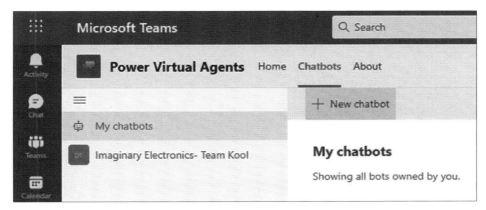

Figure 7.2 – New chatbot within Teams

You will be presented with a wizard to choose a team for this chatbot, which allows the team owners and you (the bot owner/author) to have access to it. Click **Continue** on this screen to be presented with another screen where you can see fields for the bot's name and language.

You can alternatively launch a new chatbot from the Power Apps **Build** hub, as shown in the following screenshot:

Figure 7.3 – New chatbot from the Build hub

3. Enter a name that you like and choose the language. For illustration purposes, I chose to name this chatbot Nostradamus and set **English (US)** as the language.

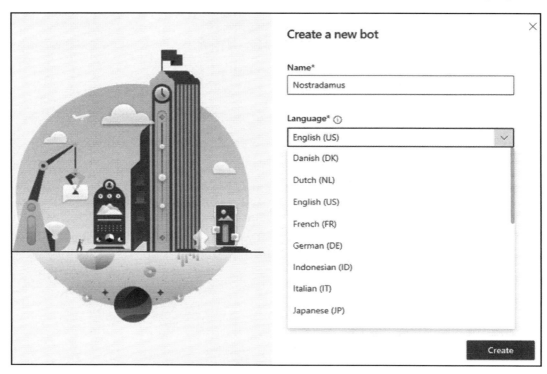

Figure 7.4 – Creating a new chatbot

4. Click **Create** to continue. You will see an animation of a robot doing some background work before eventually landing on a page, as shown in the following screenshot:

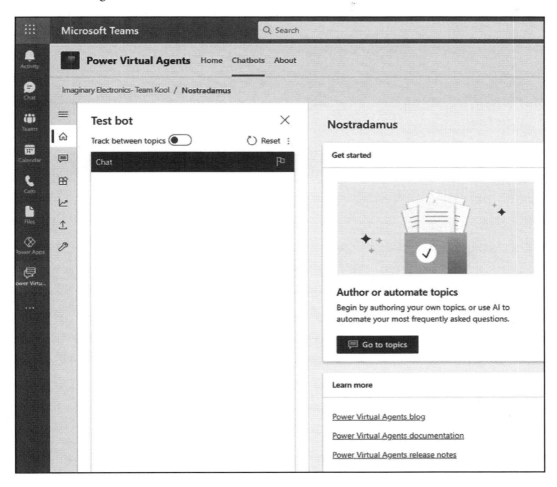

Figure 7.5 – Starting page after bot initiation

5. Click the **Go to topics** button to land on the page where topics are authored. You will see that PVA has already provided some out-of-the-box topics that are commonly used, as seen in the following screenshot. You will see that there are some commonly used topics such as **Greeting**, **Goodbye**, and **Thank you**. While we can use some of these out-of-the-box topics in our bot, we still need to create a new custom topic where we will write custom logic to handle our scenario with Health Scanner:

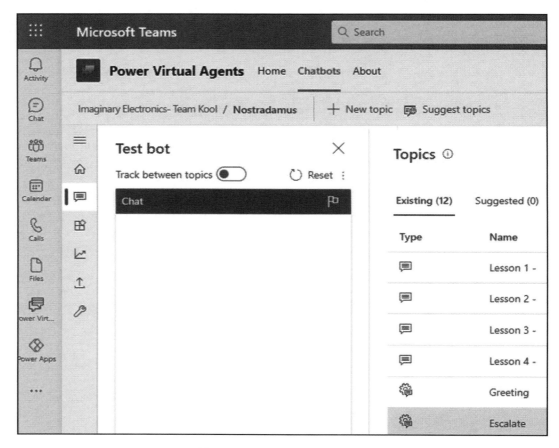

Figure 7.6 – Existing topics page

6. Click on the **New topic** option to get started with authoring a new topic that will focus on our scenario around the Health Scanner app. This leads to the setup screen, as illustrated in the following screenshot, where we can add trigger phrases. Let's type in some phrases, such as I want help, Help Needed, and Nostradamus. We can keep adding more phrases later as we learn other commonly used phrases that end users use within the organization when looking for information:

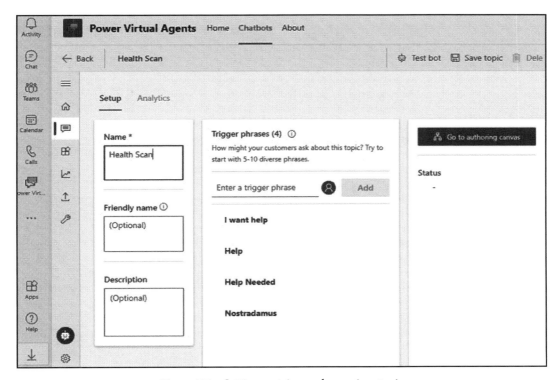

Figure 7.7 – Setting up trigger phrases in a topic

Trigger phrases

Trigger phrases are words or phrases that can be used to initiate or activate the bot, very much like voice-activated digital assistants such as Siri on your Apple iPhone, which can be invoked with "Hey Siri," Amazon's Alexa, which uses "Hey Alexa," or Google Assistant, which uses the "OK Google" or "Hey Google" commands. The only difference here is that all these digital assistants are voice-activated, whereas the trigger phrases in our chatbot here need to be typed in by the user.

7.   Next, let's go to the authoring canvas to start authoring the topic. This can be
     done by clicking the **Go to authoring canvas** button in the top-right corner of
     the screen. You will be dropped into a bot flow that has already set up the trigger
     phrases as the initial step, followed by a prompt to post a message in return. Here,
     if you click on the {**X**} icon, you will see the options to use built-in variables such as
     UserDisplayName or **UserId**. This helps you to post a customized acknowledgment
     back to the user.

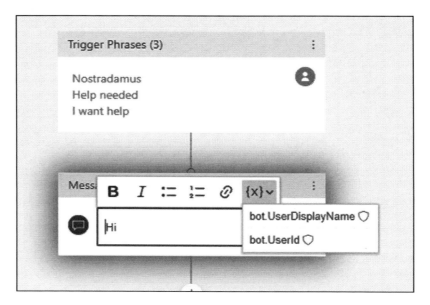

Figure 7.8 – Using built-in variables within a topic

8.   Click **bot.UserDisplayName**, as seen in the preceding screenshot, to address
     the user. This will be seen by the end user as a way of the bot acknowledging or
     responding. Once this is done, you will observe that there is a test bot provided
     on the left side of the screen. As the name suggests, this can be used to test the bot
     while you are building it. After saving the topic, by using the **Save** button on the top
     right of the screen, you can start invoking the bot by typing the trigger phrases. As
     you can see in the following screenshot, the bot will respond with the message that
     you defined in the topic:

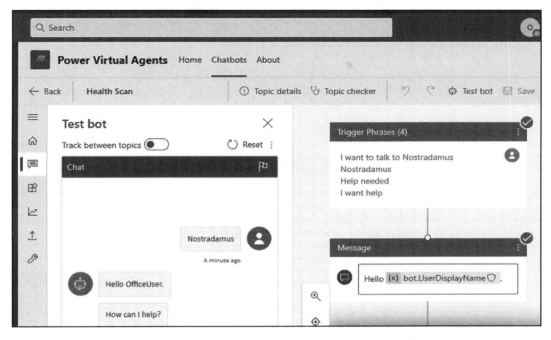

Figure 7.9 – Test bot helps with validation as you build

9. Now, using the **Add node**/(+) icon, continue adding nodes to the topic and then ask a closed-ended question.

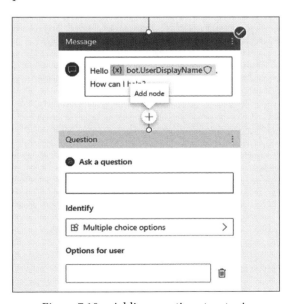

Figure 7.10 – Adding questions to a topic

10. Add two choices, as shown in the following screenshot. Note that the option chosen will be stored in a variable, which you rename `Option`. You will observe that as soon as options are added, the topic branches are created automatically:

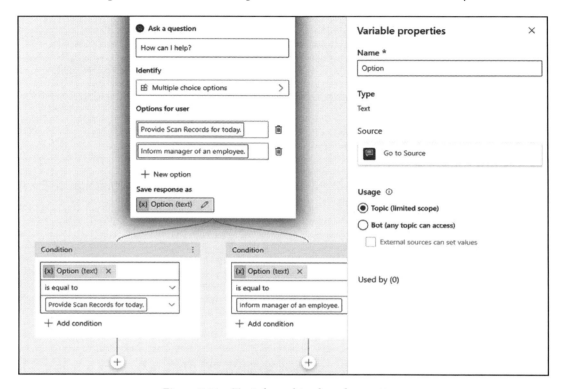

Figure 7.11 – Topic branching based on options

The branches are proportional to the number of choice options you provide, since each option can then be tailored to provide a custom response.

11. As seen in the following screenshot, you can keep adding more nodes and test them simultaneously in the test bot:

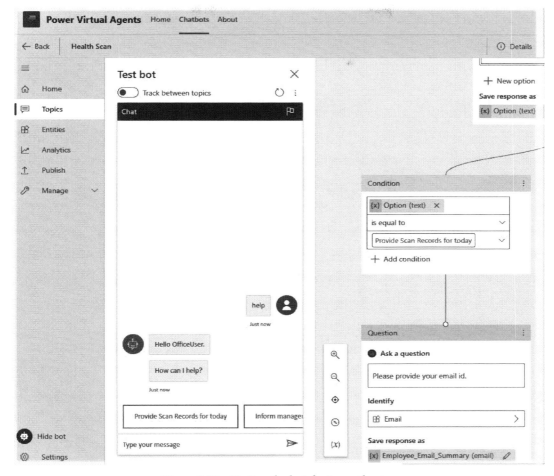

Figure 7.12 – Testing the bot during authoring

Throughout the process of authoring a bot, you can keep testing the bot using the test bot.

In this section, we have seen how to get the topic set up so that the bot will respond with preconfigured messages and questions to steer the conversation. In the next section, we will see how the bot can be configured to act on these choices with preconfigured actions, by leveraging the flows that we built earlier, in the previous chapter.

Adding flows to Power Virtual Agent bot

In this section, we will add more nodes that can act based on the user's selection of choices that we configured in the bot. In the following steps, you will see how a Power Automate flow can be invoked in response to the choices presented to the user:

1. Select the **Inform manager of an employee** option and click **Add node** (represented by the + icon). Then, click the **Call an action** option, which will present the option to create a flow, as shown in the following screenshot:

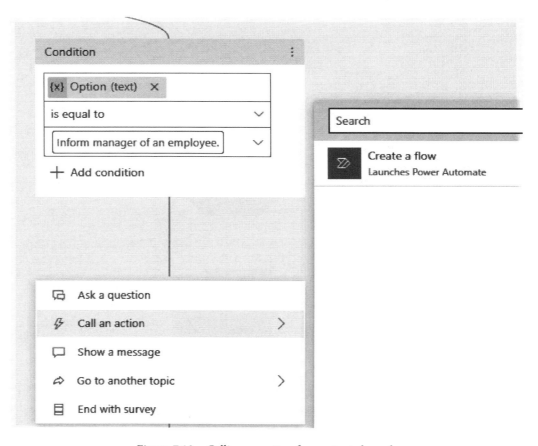

Figure 7.13 – Calling an action from a topic branch

2. This will take you to another screen where there are a few instant flow templates, as seen in the following screenshot. Let's pick the template with the name **Power Virtual Agents Flow Template**:

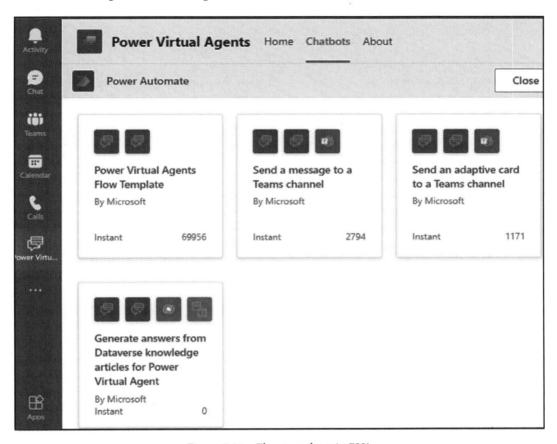

Figure 7.14 – Flow templates in PVA

Once the template is selected, you land on a familiar-looking screen, which is the Power Automate flow editor with two steps prepopulated for you, as seen in the following screenshot. The first one will help you choose how to grab a value from the user through the bot, to be used as a parameter within the flow. The second variable in the second step will be used to pass the result back to the bot:

Figure 7.15 – Passing values between the bot and flow

3. Pick **Text** input to capture user input. This value will be an employee email address provided by the end user of the bot, which will be used to look up the manager of the employee whose email is provided – as with the instant flow that we built earlier in this chapter.

4. Name this input variable EmployeeEmail. Similarly, the output that will be required to be provided to the user of the bot will be the manager's email, so let's call the output variable ManagerEmail.

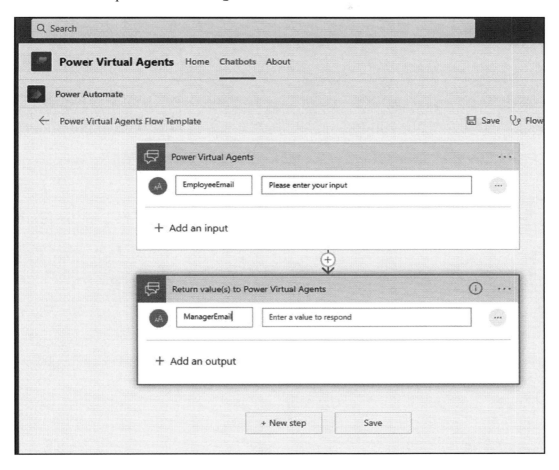

Figure 7.16 – Passing values between the bot and flow

5. Now, using the new step (+) icon in between the two PVA steps, add an intermediate step, which will use the Office 365 connector and fetch the manager details, as shown in the following screenshot:

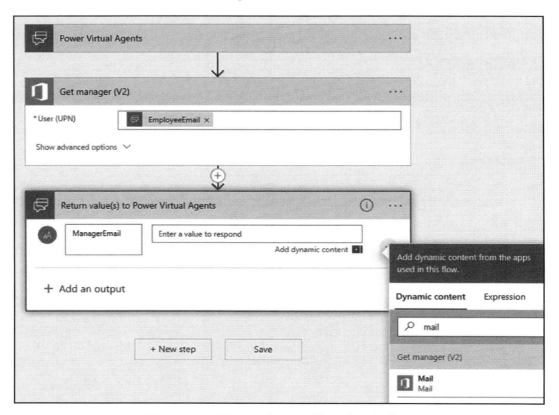

Figure 7.17 – Using the bot variable within the flow

Here, we used the same **Get manager (V2)** action from the Office 365 connector to fetch the manager details, just like we did in the previous example of a Power Automate instant flow. The only difference here is that the input for this flow step is the **EmployeeEmail** variable obtained from the bot user in the previous PVA step. In the instant flow example, it was obtained from the app, based on the selected employee needing attention, and then invoked through a button named **Notify**. Similarly, we will use the **Mail** output to store the manager's email in the **ManagerEmail** variable so that it is available as a response from the bot to the user of the bot.

6. In the next step, add a **Send an email** step with a custom message. Also, add **BotUser** as additional input within the first step of the Power Automate flow. This **BotUser** can then be used to let the manager know who from the medical team initiated the email. See the **BotUser** variable used at the bottom of the email body in the following screenshot:

Figure 7.18 – Using more than one variable input in a topic

7. As seen in the top-left corner of the preceding screenshot, we ensure the name of the flow, **Power Virtual Agents Flow Template**, is changed to something meaningful and distinguishable, such as **InformManager**, and then we are ready to save and test this flow. You will observe that this flow cannot be triggered for testing independently. This is fine; we will test it when the entire bot is ready for testing.

8. Close the flow authoring using the **Close** button on the top right of the screen. This will take you back to the **Topic authoring** canvas, where you will add an additional question as a node under the selection option to seek the email address of the employee whose manager needs to be informed.

    As seen in the following screenshot, you can add a question and seek the response to be validated using the **Identify** field. The **Identify** field uses built-in logic to identify emails and other such real-world entities, such as age, city, or color, that the PVA bot platform is aware of. For the sake of differentiating from the EmployeeEmail input that we used in the flow, here we will save the response as Employee_Email:

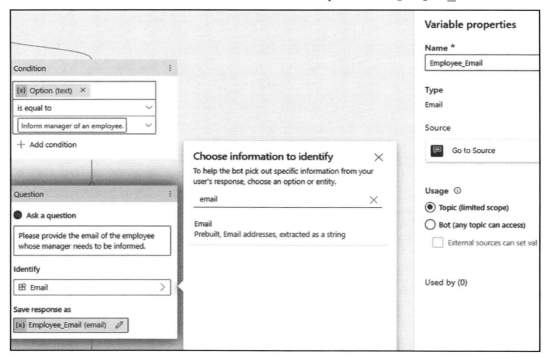

Figure 7.19 – Capturing output from the bot and storing it in a variable

9.   Add the Power Automate **GetManagerEmail** flow as the next action under the selected condition node/step (**Inform manager of an employee**) in the bot.

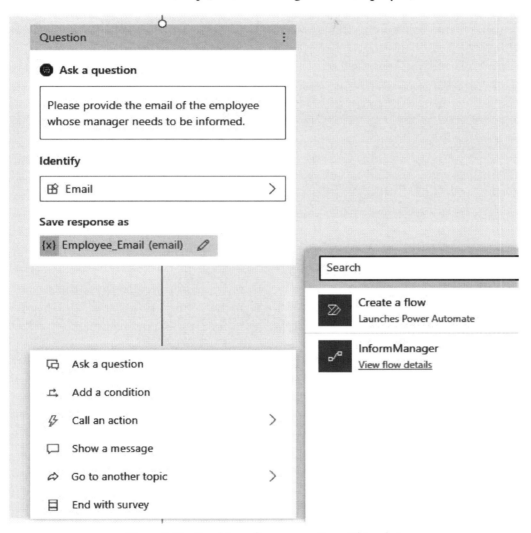

Figure 7.20 – Invoking a flow as an action within a bot

10. Once the flow is added as a step, you will be prompted to provide the two inputs that the **InformManager** flow expects – **EmployeeEmail** and **BotUser**. The **EmployeeEmail** value can be obtained from the **Employee_Email** value that we got as a response from the bot user and **BotUser** can be obtained from the bot platform, which is automatically available as **bot.UserDisplayName** and **bot.UserId**. We will use **bot.UserDisplayName** for this scenario.

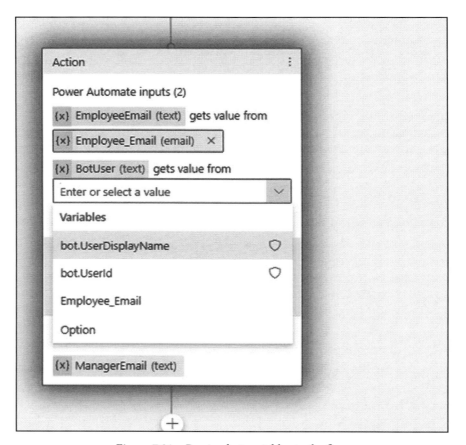

Figure 7.21 – Passing bot variables to the flow

11. Add the final steps to post an acknowledgment to the user that the manager of this employee was informed using the **Show a message** option. Here, you can leverage the **ManagerEmail** output from the flow to show the email ID of the manager who was informed as part of the flow action. Similarly, you can use **Go to another topic** to use out-of-the-box topics such as **End of Conversation** or **Thank you**.

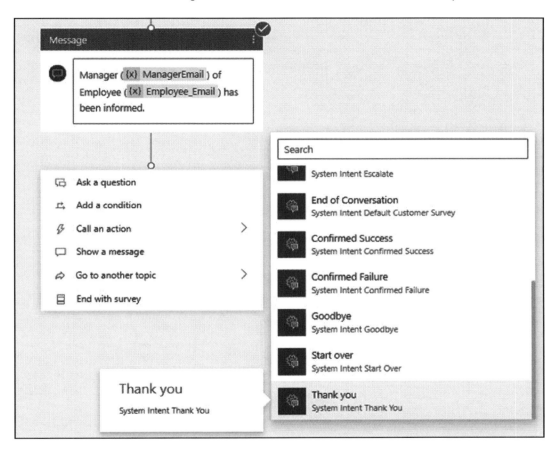

Figure 7.22 – Using out-of-the-box topics to end the conversation

12. Now it's time to use the test bot. Please see the following screenshot to see how it can be tested:

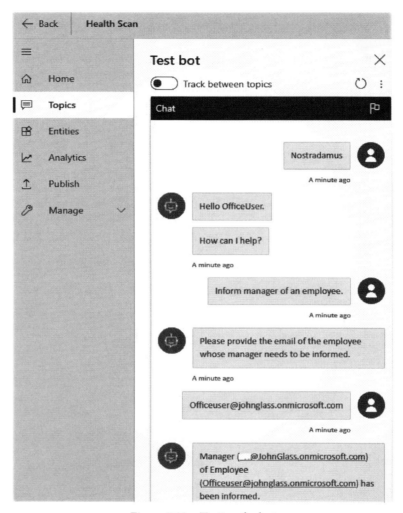

Figure 7.23 – Testing the bot

We have completed one set of actions to be taken when the bot user chooses the **Inform manager of an employee** option, where we forked the bot response. Now we need to build the response for the other option, which was **Provide Scan Records for today**.

13. Next, we will add a step to seek the email ID of the employee to whom the daily summary email needs to be sent. Save this response from the end user as the `Employee_Email_Summary` variable.

14. Following this, add a **Call an action** step to wire up another Power Automate flow.

    This flow can be authored exactly like the **Scheduled** flow we built in the previous section. The following screenshot shows how the **GetDailySummary** flow was authored before wiring it as an action into the bot. In the following screenshot, all the steps are the same as we built in the scheduled daily summary flow in the previous section:

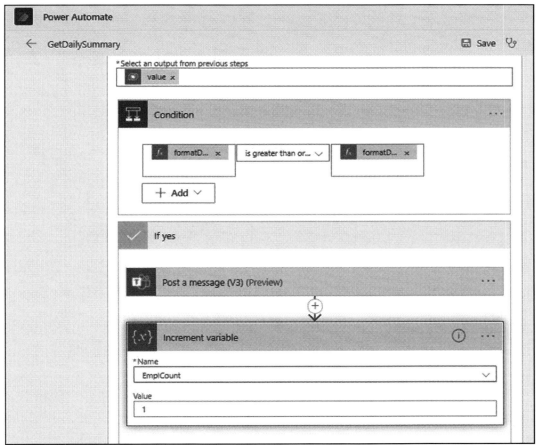

Figure 7.24 – Using Initialize variable and Set variable actions within a flow

The only difference here is that we used the PVA template to initialize it and then used an **EmplCount** variable to increment the count of employees needing attention, every time the conditions are met, the first filter being body temperature greater than 99 and then the second condition being a scan date greater than yesterday.

As of the time of writing, the Power Automate flow action cannot automatically loop through and output the result back to the bot when multiple values are returned from a step within the flow. This is the reason why, in this example, we gather the bot user's email and send the daily summary in an email asynchronously and just report the count of employees (**EmplCount**) as a summary.

> **Actions related to variables**
>
> There are a few useful actions such as **Set variable** and **Increment variable**, as seen in the preceding screenshot, that can be used to temporarily hold a value that can be passed between steps. Such value holders, such as **EmplCount**, known as a **variable**, need to be initialized in one of the previous steps, as seen in the **Initialize variable** step.

15. Finally, test this option of the bot response, as shown in the following screenshot, using the test bot:

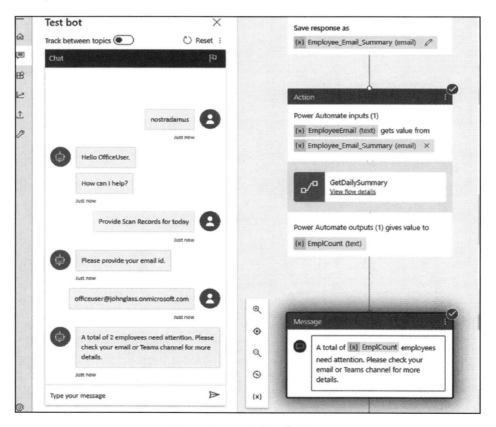

Figure 7.25 – Testing the bot

This concludes building the topic for the Health Scanner application. In the next section, we will see how to test this topic from within a bot and publish the bot.

Publishing the Power Virtual Agent bot

In the previous section, we saw how the topic can be authored with different flows and it is time to now test the bot end to end, like a real-world user would, for both the options using the test bot, and then publish it for consumption by the end users. You will observe that the bot brings into play all the out-of-the-box topics such as greetings that you didn't author, thus helping you to take care of often-used conversations and automatic responses. Let's start the steps to publish the bot for consumption by the end users, which could be your team or the entire organization:

1. Navigate to the PVA icon on the Teams rail on the left and click the **Chatbots** option on the menu, and you will see the **Nostradamus** chatbot.

2. Click the bot and you will see the test bot and the **Publish bot** button. Click **Publish bot**:

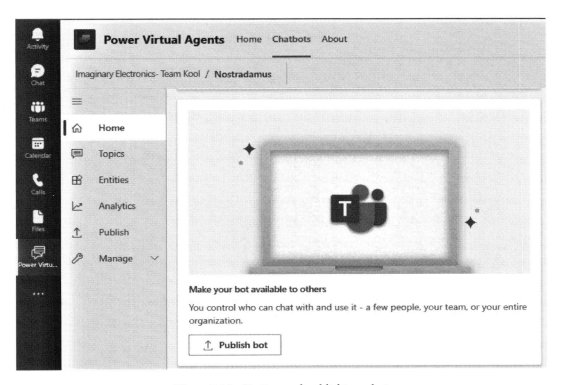

Figure 7.26 – Testing and publishing a bot

3. It takes a few minutes for the bot to be published. After few minutes, once the bot is published, you can open it from the same page or use the PVA option on the Teams rail, followed by the **Chatbots** menu, and then click the bot (named Nostradamus).

You will see two options to open the bot. Clicking on **Open the bot** will prompt you to add it to the Teams rail, as shown in the following screenshot:

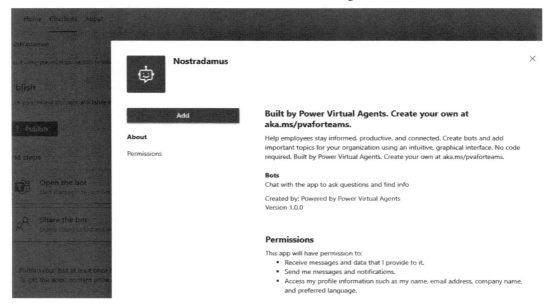

Figure 7.27 – Adding the bot to the Teams rail, after publishing

If you choose the second option, **Share the bot**, then you will see two more options for sharing: **Share with my organization**, which shares the bot to be used by the entire organization, and **Share with my team**. Selecting the **Share with my organization** option will submit the bot for approval by the admin of your organization, who could either approve or reject the bot. On approval by the admin, you can open the bot and share the link of the approved version of your bot with anyone in your organization. Choosing the **Share with my team** option will enable you to share the bot with members of the Microsoft Teams that you choose.

PVA in Teams is an evolving area and may see changes in the steps or user interfaces provided in the preceding screenshots. Please refer to `https://docs.microsoft.com/en-us/power-virtual-agents/teams/publication-fundamentals-publish-channels-teams` to stay updated on the latest version, especially for the publishing steps.

4. For illustration in this book, we have chosen the **Add to Teams** option; you will see the bot appearing on the Microsoft Teams rail to the left, with its name.

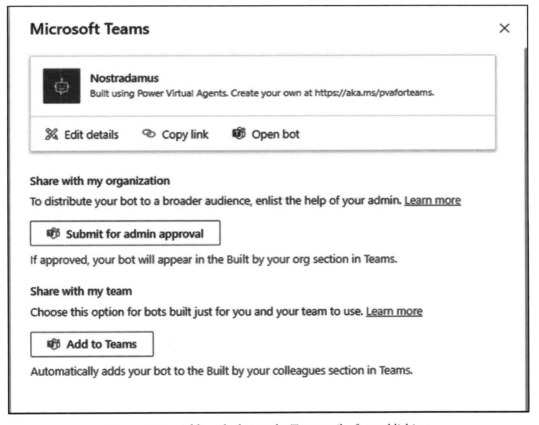

Figure 7.28 – Adding the bot to the Teams rail, after publishing

5. Next, as seen in the following screenshot, you can carry out end-to-end testing of the bot by ensuring that it is responding to all questions and choices selected by the end user.

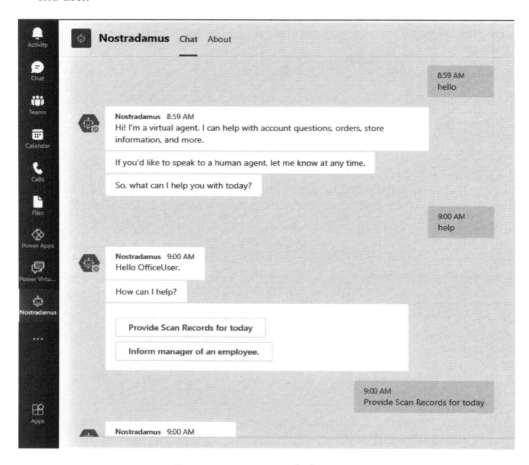

Figure 7.29 – Bot is ready for action

You can continue to extend the Nostradamus bot by adding more topics incrementally, as the requirements continue to emerge organically.

In this section, we have seen the various options of publishing, such as publishing the bot for consumption by users of your team or publishing it to the entire organization. Publishing the chatbot for consumption by the entire organization does need your organization's Teams administrator to approve the app. If you are the Teams administrator in your organization, you can see the different apps and bots submitted for approval. The Teams administrator can refer to this link, https://docs.microsoft.com/en-us/microsoftteams/manage-apps, to learn more about how to manage these different apps and bots.

Summary

In this chapter, we have seen different aspects of PVA, such as how to author a chatbot using topics as building blocks. We also saw how commonly used topics, such as greetings, which are provided out of the box, help us to get natural conversations going with the bot. We learned how within each topic, you can ask a question with multiple choices for users to respond, how to trigger a preconfigured action using Power Automate flows, how to create and use variables, and how to leverage out-of-the-box system variables such as **UserDisplayName**. We also saw how variables can be leveraged to pass values from the PVA bot to Power Automate flows and capture the response from the flow execution back into the PVA bot. We built a bot that helped us to automate repeatable actions, such as sending a summary or tasks such as informing the manager of an employee who needs attention, as well as answering questions such as the number of employees who need attention that day. Using the example illustrated in this chapter, you will be able to share information for many such repeatedly asked questions or carry out preconfigured tasks by leveraging the power of PVA.

In the next chapter, we will look at how the application life cycle is maintained for business-critical applications. The process involves building apps, bots, and flows in a test environment where they are built and tested by developers and testers. Once testing is complete and a certain quality threshold is met, these apps, bots, and flows are moved into another environment, often referred to as the production or live environment, where end users of these applications will start using it.

Section 3: Application and Environment Life Cycle Management

While building apps for production use, it is important to leverage the life cycle management practices required for creation, migration, maintenance, decommissioning, and more. Power Apps, Power Virtual Agents bots, and Power Automate flows can be packaged as a single deployable unit, or solution. Besides the versions of the applications, the data and other metadata that is stored in the environment (along with Dataverse) might need to be migrated from time to time, especially when dev/test environments have to be separated from the production version/environment. Similarly, these environments also need provisioning, backup, restore, and decommissioning, which is all supported by Dataverse for Teams. This section also covers scenarios where an upgrade from Dataverse for Teams to Dataverse would be needed and provides step-by-step instructions for this upgrade.

This section comprises the following chapters:

- *Chapter 8, Managing the Application Life Cycle and Environment Life Cycle*
- *Chapter 9, Upgrading to Microsoft Dataverse Environment*

8
Managing the Application Life Cycle and Environment Life Cycle

In the previous chapter, we looked at how a **Power Virtual Agents** (**PVA**) chatbot can be created to help with addressing the most frequently asked questions. We also learned how Power Automate flows can be integrated with a PVA chatbot to trigger business tasks without writing a single line of code. We must now look at the next set of challenges that comes while deploying these apps, bots, and flows into a production environment, especially when you have a few thousand or million end users using these solutions.

In this chapter, we will learn about the application and environment life cycles, which will help us to overcome these challenges with ease. Here are the topics that we will cover in this chapter:

- Understanding Environments
- Power Platform Admin Center
- Environment Life Cycle Operations
- Application Life Cycle Management

By the end of this chapter, you will have learned how to manage different types of environments. Also, you will know how to package your applications, bots, and flows, and promote them from test environments to production environments, where end users would be able to use these artifacts.

In the first section of this chapter, we will start with understanding what an environment is and how and why it is important to us while building power apps, bots, and flows.

Understanding Environments

In this section, we will start with a basic understanding of an environment, and the different types of environments that you will see in the Power Platform. We'll also learn how Dataverse for Teams environments are different from other types of Power Platform environments. To begin with, let's refresh what we learned about environments in *Chapter 2, Exploring Microsoft Dataverse for Teams*; that is, an **environment** is like a virtual container for all parts of the Power Platform that are logically related, dependent on the same set of data, or just co-located for business reasons. Today, in Dataverse for Teams, there is a one-to-one mapping of each Dataverse instance backing a Teams environment.

Let's also revisit the topic of the application management life cycle that we were introduced to in *Chapter 5, Understanding Microsoft Dataverse*, where we got to know how sandbox environments (used for development and test purposes) are a crucial element in maintaining healthy **Application Life Cycle Management** (**ALM**). This life cycle can be seen in the following figure:

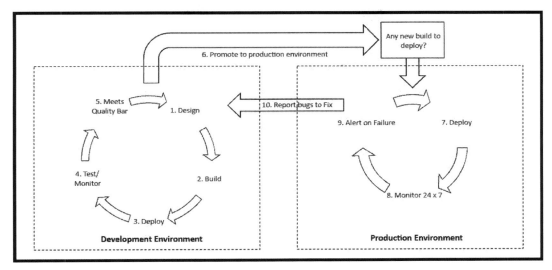

Figure 8.1 – Application management life cycle

As seen in the preceding figure, the process starts with the ideation and design phase of the app, bot, or flow, followed by building, testing, deployment, and then monitoring in the dev/test environment. If there are no bugs found in the dev/test environment, this stable version of the app, flow, or bot is promoted into the production environment. This environment is now a container for the apps, flows, and bots that you have built so far. Besides concerns about mixing up test versus production users of your app, if you think about the whole organization, there will be various groups or departments and there might be a need to keep these boundaries logically separated from each other. This means within a company, represented as a Microsoft **Azure Active Directory (AAD)** tenant, you could create as many environments as possible to logically keep the data and applications grouped together for business or other strategic reasons. There are a few different types of these environments that are created in Power Platform. They are as follows:

- Production
- Sandbox
- Default
- Trial
- Developer
- Microsoft Dataverse for Teams

Let's take a quick look at each of these different types of environments.

Production Environment

A production environment is an environment where you push the best version of apps, flows, and bots after they have been tested and deemed to be ready for consumption by the end users of the application. These environments have additional features, such as disaster recovery enabled and backup history for a much longer time than a sandbox environment. Other environment operations, such as copy (to clone a copy for testing) and delete, are also supported for this production environment.

Sandbox Environment

A sandbox environment is an environment that should be used for testing and validation. This environment, being different and isolated from production environments, is a safe place to try out new changes without impacting the end users. These environments have limited features, such as no active disaster recovery and short backup history. However, a sandbox can be completely reset; that is, you can wipe out all the customizations and data and reset it as a new environment if needed to start a fresh cycle of testing. You can also make copies of this environment to carry out other activities in parallel, if needed.

Default Environment

The default environment is a special type of production environment that is created automatically by the platform to enable a lot of first-run experiences for Power Apps, Power Automate, and PVA. There is a single default environment per organization, that is, **Azure Active Directory** (**AAD**) tenant, and all users in this tenant are automatically given the privilege of being a maker (customizer) in this environment. This means that all users in this tenant can make apps, bots, and flows within the default environment without the need to be given permissions by their administrator. Since this default environment is created automatically and is meant for a first-use experience, there are a few limitations; for example, you can't perform usual environment life cycle operations such as delete, backup, and restore on this default environment.

Trial Environment

Trial environments can be provisioned by administrators for short-term evaluation needs and as the name suggests, they are not meant for production use. These environments expire at the end of 30 days from the day it was created and are usually limited to a single user.

Developer Environment

These environments can be created by users with a Developer plan license. These environments are not meant to be used by more than one person, that is, the person who created the environment. They are usually created by individuals to test some features or for personal training purposes.

More information about the Developer plan license can be found at `https://docs.microsoft.com/en-us/powerapps/maker/developer-plan`.

Microsoft Dataverse for Teams

Microsoft Dataverse for Teams provides environments that are automatically created for the corresponding team where apps, bots, or flows are created, as we learned in previous chapters. It is tightly bound to the Microsoft Teams experience, hence the life cycle and related operations are managed through Microsoft Teams.

Now that we have different types of environments, let's see how we can leverage some of these environment operations. However, before we look at environment operations, let's get a quick overview of the **Power Platform Admin Center** (**PPAC**), which is where all administrative operations related to Power Platform can be performed. In the next section, we will look at the PPAC and the various capabilities available in the PPAC.

Power Platform Admin Center

In this section, we will see various aspects of the Power Platform administration experience that are provided in the PPAC. You will be able to use the admin center by navigating to `https://admin.powerplatform.microsoft.com/`. There are a few subsections on the PPAC and in this section, we will take a quick tour of each of these subsections. Let's start with the first one, which is a list of environments, and also the landing page for PPAC.

On the **Environments** page, you will be able to see all the different types of environments that we saw in the preceding section. As seen in the following screenshot, it will have additional details for each of these environments, such as **State**, **Region**, **Created on**, and **Created by**. As the name suggests, **State** represents the current life cycle state of the environment. Some of the common states that you will come across are **Provisioning**, **Ready**, **Disabled**, and **Deleted**.

The **Provisioning** state is shown just after you kickstart environment creation using the **New** button. The **Ready** state signifies the environment is ready for use, while the **Disabled** state is usually shown after the trial period has expired and the environment is pending deletion. Environments in the **Deleted** state will have the state as **Deleted**; however, deleted environments are often moved to a different page, which can be viewed at `https://admin.powerplatform.microsoft.com/environments/deleted`. Since there is not much to do with deleted environments other than to recover them, this page is often not shown unless you have any environments that can be recovered:

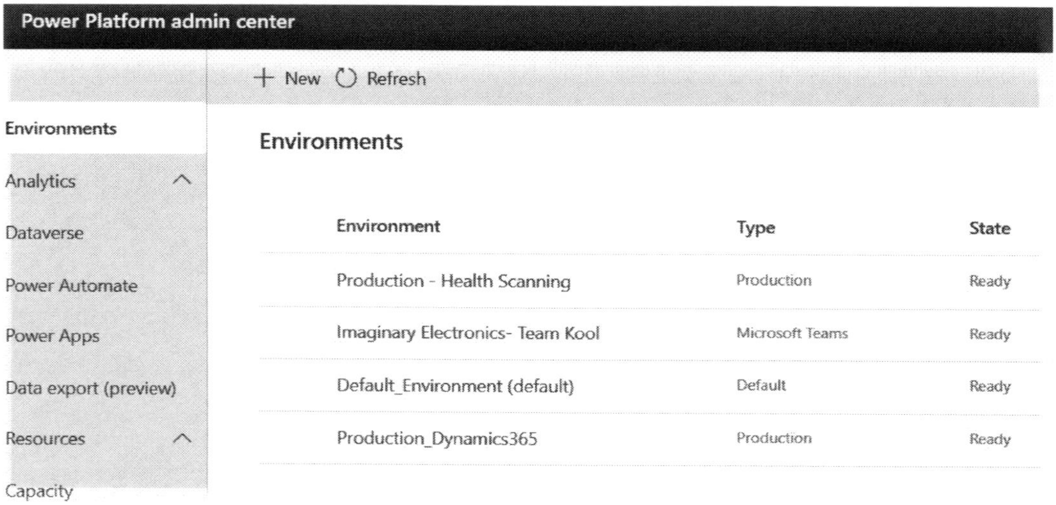

Figure 8.2 – Environments in the PPAC

There is another section in the PPAC that covers analytics data for Power Apps, Power Automate, and Dataverse. We saw in *Chapter 4, Enhancing Your App with Images, Screens, and File Attachments*, how analytics of an app provide insights on the usage of our app. Similarly, there are analytics on Power Automate flows and Dataverse usage in this section.

Another section to look at is the **Resources** section, which is where you will find the capacity information about different types of environments. As you can see in the following screenshot, there are a few subsections here to look at capacity consumption by different components such as Dataverse, Microsoft Teams environments, and trials. This is where you get to see the number of environments used and the total storage (GB) used in these environments. If you are using Power Apps and Dataverse outside of the Teams environment, there is also a section to see capacity consumption from standalone usage of Dataverse and Power Apps:

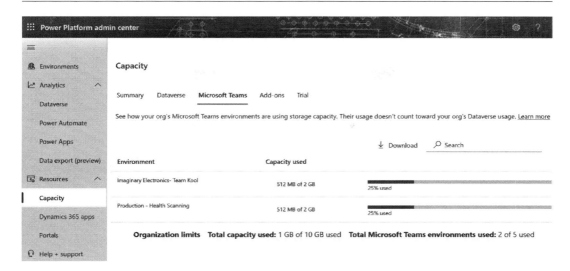

Figure 8.3 – Capacity information in the PPAC

There is a **Help + support** section in the PPAC that can be used to create a new support request for Microsoft.

There are additional configuration pages in the PPAC, such as **Data integration**, **Data**, and **Data policies**, which are still evolving – both from a feature and a PPAC experience perspective. The goal of these sections is to provide administrative experience for configuring the data integration feature. The data integration feature allows your organization to share its data with external systems of your choice. Similarly, data policies help the administrator to configure policies for **Data Loss Prevention** (**DLP**). DLP policies allow administrators to block certain types of data connectors to be used with the tenant, whereby users within the tenant will be blocked from using a particular type of connector within their app, and they prevent sensitive business information/data from being exposed or leaked.

> **Note about Power Platform admin center**
> As Power Platform grows, new administration requirements will be added. The preceding section was focused on some important scenarios that you will need to be aware of, especially while using Dataverse for Teams.

Thus, we can see that the PPAC is the place for all administrative operations and analytics that you would need while using Power Platform. In the next section, we will see how we can leverage the PPAC to carry out various life cycle operations in the context of a Microsoft Dataverse for Teams environment.

Environment life cycle Operations

In this section, we will look at some of the important environment life cycle operations that you may need to use, such as backup, restore, and delete operations. Let's start with the backup operation and then see how these backed-up instances can be restored.

Environment Backup and Restore

Environment backups are automatically taken by the platform every 10 to 15 minutes. However, when you wish to create a named/labeled backup (as markup) to remember a point in time that you want to bookmark, this can be done by creating manual backups. Let's see the steps to get this done:

1. Navigate to the PPAC (`https://admin.powerplatform.microsoft.com`). Here, under the **Environments** option on the left of the screen, you will see all your environments listed.

2. Choose the Dataverse for Teams environment where you wish to create a manual backup. This will open a screen that has environment details such as the type, region, and recent operations.

3. On this environment details screen, click the **Backups** option on the top menu, followed by **Create** in the drop-down option under it. This will open a slide-out panel to the right of the screen where you can put the label name and notes for your reference, as seen in the following screenshot:

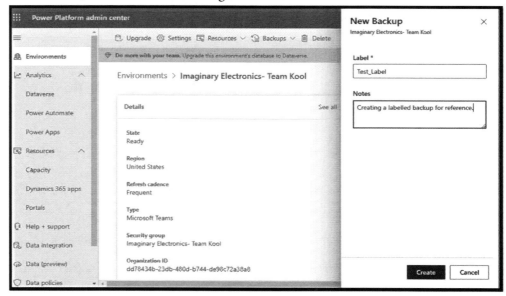

Figure 8.4 – Creating manual backups

4. Once the details are entered, click the **Create** button, after which you will see a notification message at the top of the screen, pointing you to the location where these backups are created and maintained. You can also get to this location, where manual backups are maintained, by clicking on the **Restore or manage** drop-down option under the **Backups** option on the top menu.

5. Once you are on the screen that shows manual backups, click the **Restore** or **Delete** option in the dropdown, as seen in the following screenshot:

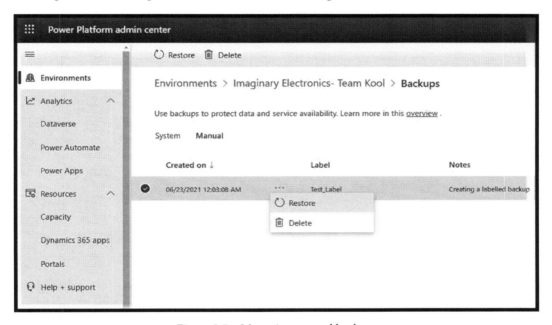

Figure 8.5 – Managing manual backups

In the preceding screenshot, you will see that you have the option to restore the manual backup that you created or an existing system-generated backup.

6. On clicking the **Restore** option, you will see a prompt to overwrite the environment with the selected backup, as seen in the following screenshot:

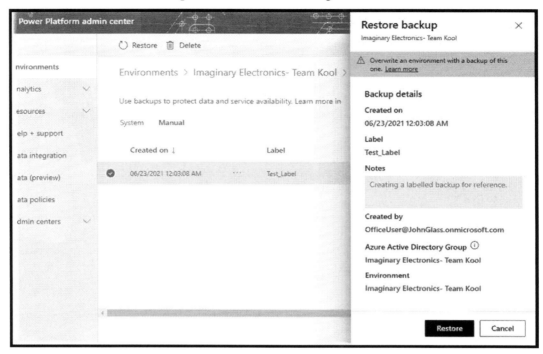

Figure 8.6 – Restoring manual backups

7. Click the **Restore** button to continue, and you will be presented with a warning informing you about the consequence of this action; that is, the environment's data will be completely deleted and replaced as part of this operation. However, the previous backups of the environment taken by the system and any manual backups will remain available.

8. Click the **Confirm** button to continue and then you will observe that the restoration process starts, and you will be able to see the progress on the screen, as seen in the following screenshot:

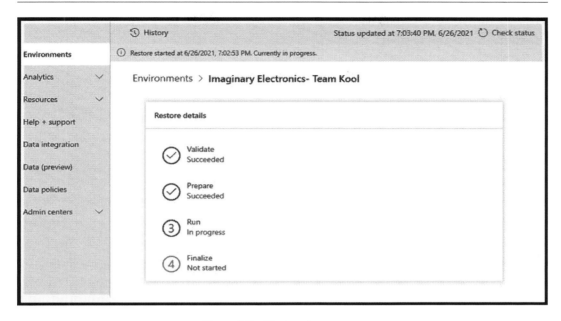

Figure 8.7 – Restore in progress

9. Once the restoration is complete, you will see a confirmation message – **Environment was restored at \<date & time of restoration\>** – as seen in the following screenshot:

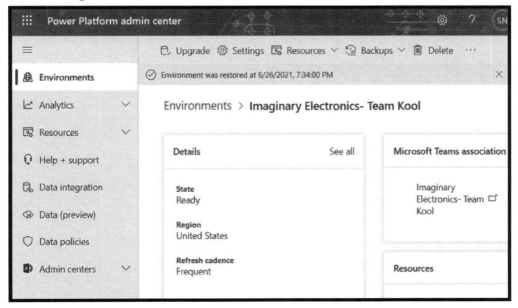

Figure 8.8 – Restore completed

> **Note**
>
> When you restore a backup, as seen in the warning messages on the screen, all the changes to apps, bots, flows, and tables that were made within the environment between the time of the snapshot chosen for backup and the current time will be lost. The only way to restore some of these changes would be to restore another system-generated backup that is close enough to the date and time desired.

Since restoring an environment is quite disruptive and there could be potential data loss, it is advised to use caution while doing this operation. Additionally, since apps support different versions, it is advised to explore options such as restoring the app versions first, before deciding to restore the environment. However, the environment restore option could be useful when you wish to restore the watermark with data in tables, reset a testing cycle back to where you started the current cycle, and so on. Since tables don't have version history, this also helps in cases where the test cases are meant to delete the data and you wish to get back to the original state before the test commenced. It is because of these reasons and scenarios that you will see that the restore option is more often used in sandbox environments than production. With Dataverse for Teams, these backup and restoration operations only act on the data inside Dataverse for Teams; that is, only apps, bots, flows, and tables within the Dataverse for Teams environment are backed up and restored, while changes made to Microsoft Teams, such as changes to the team name, are not backed up or are not restorable through these operations in the PPAC. Let's look at some other environment operations that are not used so often, and you will see why they should be used with caution.

Environment Delete

You will use this operation to delete any environment that you have access to within the PPAC. Once an environment is deleted, you will lose all the apps, bots, tables, and flows associated with it. Due to the risky consequences of this operation, you are always asked to confirm the deletion by typing in the name of the environment before deletion is carried out by the platform. However, you will also have 7 days to recover this environment if this was done by mistake. You can see the **Delete** option in the top menu, as seen in *Figure 8.8*, next to other environment operations, such as **Upgrade** and **Backups**.

There is a one-to-one mapping with Microsoft Teams that is connected to Dataverse for Teams environments and this Dataverse for Teams environment also gets deleted if the Teams account related to this environment is deleted.

Environment Copy

The environment copy operation is used to clone an entire environment along with the apps and data into another sandbox environment. With the copy operation, you will have two sub-options – copy everything (Customizations, Schema, and data) or just the customizations and schema. Copying everything helps you to make an exact clone of the production environment in cases where you would like to do full regression testing. However, sometimes, due to large volumes of production data or privacy concerns with duplicating business-critical and **Personally Identifiable Information** (PII) data, only customizations and the schema are copied. Test or sample data is generated later to help bridge the gap for testing. Large volumes of data cause environment sizes to increase and hence you may run out of the storage capacity allotted to your tenant, requiring you to purchase additional platform storage – which is an option we will explore in the chapter related to licensing. However, for security and privacy reasons, most organizations restrict access to production environments to a very limited set of folks and in such cases, using a copy based on the customization and schema makes sense for testing needs.

Environment reset

Environment reset is an operation that combines the power to delete and create a new environment into a single operation. This option has all the same effects as that of a delete operation, mentioned in an earlier section. Reset is mostly used to remove unwanted data from an environment and restart a test cycle.

> **Note about Teams environments**
>
> The **Copy** and **Reset** operations are not available on Teams environments since they are closely mapped to a Microsoft Team and hence allowing these operations would cause misalignment with the corresponding Microsoft Teams life cycle. The **Delete** operation is supported for Teams environments and can be deleted by a Microsoft Teams owner, and similarly, a Teams environment will be deleted automatically if the Microsoft Teams instance it was created in is deleted. Similarly, **Upgrade** is an option available only for Teams environments so that you can convert it into an environment of the production or sandbox type, backed by Dataverse instead of Dataverse for Teams.

We have now seen how to leverage environment life cycle operations in various scenarios, such as backing up an environment, restoring these environments, copying an environment, and deleting them when not needed. In the next section, we will look at how to manage the life cycle of an application.

Application Life cycle Management

In this section, we are going to see various aspects of an application's life cycle and how they can be managed. ALM is a very broad subject and, for the purpose of this book and the intended audience, we will cover the basic aspects needed by a citizen developer to build an application and maintain and govern various application components and properties.

ALM for Power Platform hinges on three core elements, which are **solutions**, **Dataverse**, and the **source control repository**. Let's see how these elements help with ALM in the following sections.

Solutions

As seen in *Chapter 5, Understanding Microsoft Dataverse*, of this book, all the application changes, along with metadata changes and customizations done to components of Microsoft Dataverse, are packaged into what is called **solutions**. You can compare solutions to installables such as `.msi`, `.app`, or `.exe`, or any application that you usually download from a public marketplace and install on your computer. Once you create an application, with apps, flows, and schema (table definition for entities within Microsoft Dataverse), all these components should be packaged as a solution. This solution file, which contains all the interdependent changes, can then be deployed to another testing or production environment, as needed.

Solutions can be of two types – managed solutions and unmanaged solutions. Let's look at them next.

Managed Solutions

Managed solutions are like certified builds that are tested, verified, and sealed to prevent any further changes. Managed solutions are used to deploy to any environment that isn't a development environment. Hence, they are used to package and export changes from a development environment and deploy them to a non-development environment for testing or production usage.

Unmanaged Solutions

App makers and developers build their apps, bots, and flows in development environments using unmanaged solutions, then import them to other test or production environments as managed solutions.

Solution Components

A solution component is any Power Platform artifact that can be packaged in a solution, for example, a Power Apps canvas app, flows, or a bot.

Now that we have learned about these solution-related topics, let's export a few components that we built in previous chapters from one Teams environment to another. This will demonstrate how you can build these components, such as apps, tables, bots, and flows, in a Teams environment designated for development, and then after testing, move it to another Teams environment where your end users can use it. This is usually done to ensure that the production environment (where end users use your apps) and its related data are not corrupted or lost during the development and testing phases.

Exporting Components

Let's see how to export all the components that you have built so far, that is, the Health Scanner app, the related table, and the Nostradamus bot that we built in the previous chapters. Follow these steps:

1. To begin with, in the **Build** hub within a Teams environment, as seen in the following screenshot, export all the components you wish to move to a different environment and hit the **Export** option at the top of the screen. This generates an **Export** fly-out panel, which provides options to include all dependencies or selected ones only. It is important to note that the platform called out that **Scan Details** was a dependent table that we forgot to include, so we should include that as well to ensure all the components have the required dependencies in the new environment to function effectively:

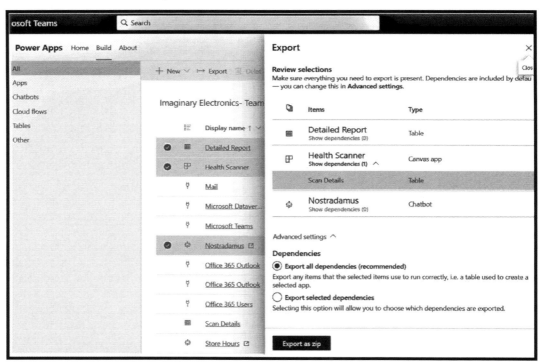

Figure 8.9 – Exporting components

2. Once you click on the **Export as zip** option, this will create the solution file with all dependencies packaged in a ZIP file. This ZIP file now contains all your solution components, which can be easily transferred to any other environment.

3. If you open/extract the ZIP file, you will see a `solution.xml` file. This `solution.xml` file contains information about all the components included in the ZIP file. In this file, as seen in the following screenshot, you will see the `<Managed>0</Managed>` string, which means that this solution was exported as an unmanaged solution. `0` here denotes false, and `1` denotes true when the solution is exported as a managed solution. In a Dataverse for Teams environment, you do not have the option of exporting as a managed solution, and to do so, you are required to create these solution components in a non-Teams environment, that is, a sandbox or production type environment, as described in an earlier section of this chapter:

```xml
<?xml version="1.0"?>
<ImportExportXml xmlns:xsi="http://www.w3.org/2001/XMLSchema-instance" generatedBy="CrmLive" languagecode="1033" SolutionPackageVersion="9.2" version="9.2.21051.140">
  <SolutionManifest>
    <UniqueName>ExportComponents3c4aa93ef54044bbb6487168c033a95e</UniqueName>
    <LocalizedNames>
      <LocalizedName languagecode="1033" description="ExportComponents3c4aa93ef54044bbb6487168c033a95e"/>
    </LocalizedNames>
    <Descriptions/>
    <Version>1.0</Version>
    <Managed>0</Managed>
    <Publisher>
      <UniqueName>Cr15b1c</UniqueName>
      <LocalizedNames>
        <LocalizedName languagecode="1033" description="CDS Default Publisher"/>
      </LocalizedNames>
      <Descriptions/>
      <EMailAddress xsi:nil="true"/>
      <SupportingWebsiteUrl xsi:nil="true"/>
      <CustomizationPrefix>crfc2</CustomizationPrefix>
      <CustomizationOptionValuePrefix>67912</CustomizationOptionValuePrefix>
    </Publisher>
    <RootComponents>
      <RootComponent behavior="0" schemaName="crfc2_detailedreport" type="1"/>
      <RootComponent behavior="0" schemaName="crfc2_scandetails" type="1"/>
      <RootComponent behavior="0" type="29" id="{38944653-8aa5-eb11-b1ac-0022481d9e61}"/>
      <RootComponent behavior="0" type="29" id="{68461864-0fa5-eb11-b1ac-0022481d9e61}"/>
      <RootComponent behavior="0" schemaName="crfc2_healthscanner_f0b49" type="300"/>
    </RootComponents>
    <MissingDependencies/>
  </SolutionManifest>
</ImportExportXml>
```

Figure 8.10 – solution.xml

This solution is now good to be imported into another Teams environment, which will be the target of your deployment, that is, a team used by your end users.

In the next section, let's import this solution into another environment that will act as our target environment.

Importing components

In this section, we will navigate to the target production environment and import the solution file that was exported in the previous section. Let's start with the following steps:

1. Create a Microsoft team at `https://admin.teams.microsoft.com/` if a production Teams environment doesn't already exist. This is exactly how we created our first team: **Imaginary Electronics- Team Kool**.

2. Next, navigate to `https://teams.microsoft.com` and click on the pinned **Power Apps** option on the Teams rail to navigate to the **Build** hub, as we did in the earlier chapters to start building new apps, bots, and so on. This will bring up a screen now with both your teams, or more, where you have access to apps, as seen in the following screenshot:

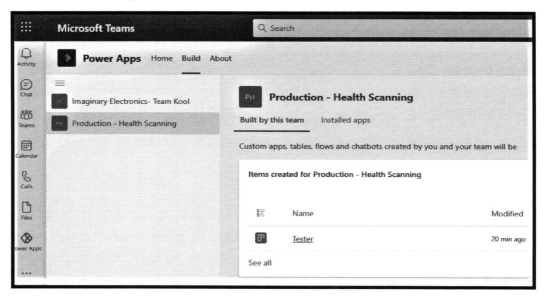

Figure 8.11 – Build hub with multiple teams

If this team is newly created, it may not be visible on the **Build** hub. In such cases, you can quickly create a sample test app from the **Home** option at the top of the screen and publish it to this new team. This will ensure that you are able to see the options to navigate to **Build** and see the **See all** option. As seen in the preceding screenshot, I created a sample app called **Tester** and published it to this new team.

3. Click the **See all** option on the screen to get to the **Build** hub of this new team – **Production - Health Scanning**.

4. Once the **Build** screen is loaded, you can click the **Import** option at the top of the screen, as seen in the following screenshot:

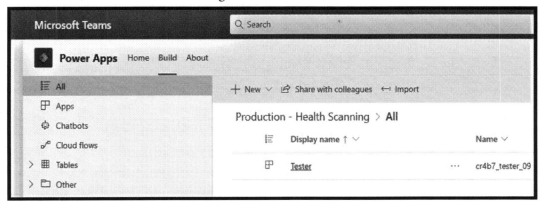

Figure 8.12 – Build hub with the Import option

5. Once you click the **Import** option, a new fly-out wizard will prompt you to select the exported ZIP (solution) file. Select this solution file that you wish to import and choose **Next**. You will see the solution file being parsed and then finally the details of the solution file will be presented, revealing the artifacts contained, which will be imported into this new environment. As seen in the following screenshot, you will have the option to deselect any component that you wish to skip in this import process:

Figure 8.13 – Import options to select and deselect components

6. Click **Next** and the wizard will now show a screen where connections contained in the solution need to be created and configured. As seen in the following screenshot, there are options to create a new connection with every data source element used in this solution, for example, Outlook to send an email, Office 365 to get users and manager information, Teams to post a message, and Microsoft Dataverse to monitor for additions or updates to Dataverse, which is used as a trigger in one of the flows contained within the solution:

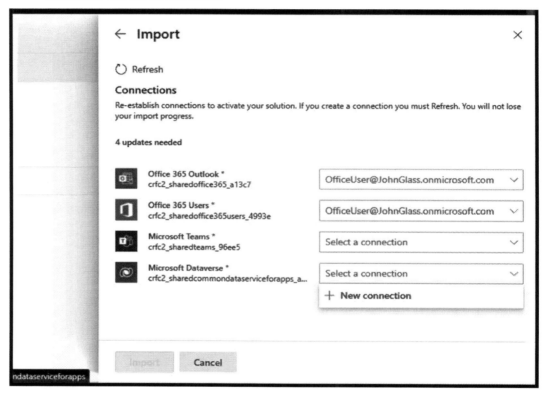

Figure 8.14 – Creating connections during import

7. To create a new connection, click on the **New connection** option, as shown in the preceding screenshot. It will open a new browser tab and take you to Power Apps Studio | **Connections** | **New connection** within the target environment. Next, as seen in the following screenshot, with Microsoft Dataverse as an example, you will be prompted to create a new connection to Microsoft Dataverse. Click **Create** to continue:

Figure 8.15 – Creating new connections to Dataverse during import

8. Meanwhile, as seen in the following screenshot, in the earlier Teams screen where the import was started, there will be a prompt to apply these new connection changes to the import wizard:

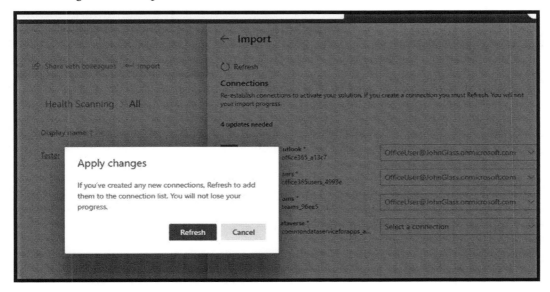

Figure 8.16 – Option to refresh connections

9. Once all new connections are created, the **Import** button gets enabled on the wizard, allowing you to continue. Click this **Import** button, as seen in the following screenshot, to start the import process:

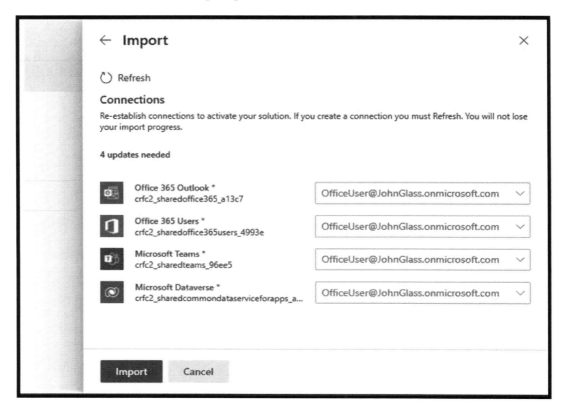

Figure 8.17 – Import enabled

10. This will initiate the import action, which is a background process, and you will see a notification message (**Currently importing customizations from the file "YourSolutionFileName.zip"**) on the screen, as seen in the following screenshot. Here, `YourSolutionFileName.zip` refers to the actual name of the ZIP file that you provided for import:

Figure 8.18 – Import in progress

This import process could take a few minutes depending on the size of the components contained in the solution file. Once the customizations are imported successfully, you will see the message change to **Customizations from the file are imported successfully**.

Once the importing is completed, you will be able to see all these newly imported solution components in the target Teams environment, that is, **Production - Health Scanning** in the case of our example, as seen in the following screenshot:

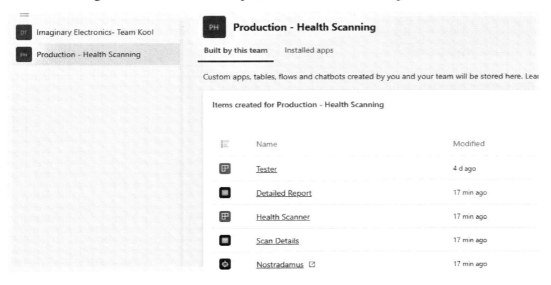

Figure 8.19 – Import completed

The final step would be to validate the app, flow, and bot in this new environment. As mentioned earlier, this new environment is like a production environment, so it would have its own set of production data or new data would be created as end users start using your app in this new environment. As seen in the following screenshot, you will be able to open this new app, add records, and publish it to your production Teams environment, as we did in the previous Teams environment:

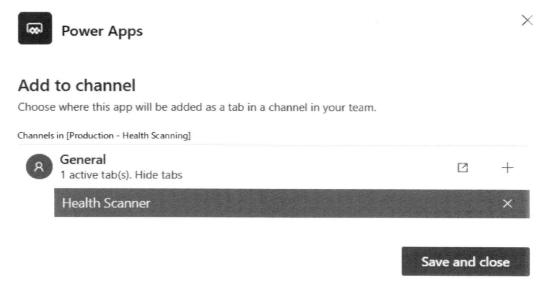

Figure 8.20 – Publishing and pinning the newly imported app

11. You can validate this by navigating to the **Production - Health Scanning** team and seeing the newly added tab – the **Health Scanner** app:

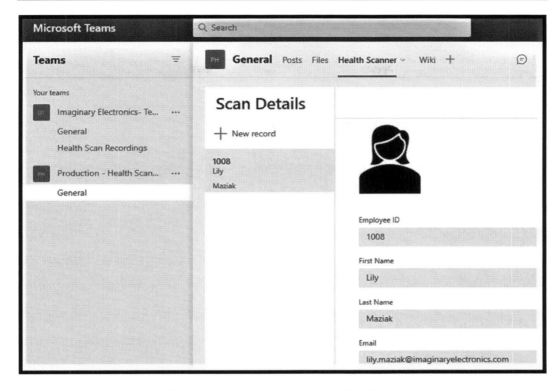

Figure 8.21 – Newly imported app in the production Teams environment

This completes the full cycle of building a solution with components such as apps, flows, bots, and tables in a dev environment and moving these components into a production or test environment as per the business needs.

Solution publisher and prefix

In the preceding screenshots, you may have observed a prefix (crfc2) in all logical names of tables and apps, for example, crfc2_detailedreport and crfc2_healthscanner_f0b49. This prefix is based on the publisher used within the environment. In a Dataverse for Teams environment, this is automatically set to the default publisher; however, in other environments, you will have the ability to create a new publisher to match your company or organization name. Most **Independent Software Vendors (ISVs)** also prefix their company names here to distinguish their solution's components easily.

For professional developers, there are many tools that can be used to manage and integrate all these changes using a source control system such as Azure DevOps (`https://docs.microsoft.com/en-us/azure/devops/user-guide/what-is-azure-devops?view=azure-devops`) into their **Continuous Integration/Continuous Deployment (CI/CD)** process.

The ALM area is continuously evolving, and you can find the latest guidance on changes related to new capabilities at `https://docs.microsoft.com/en-us/power-platform/alm/`. However, we have covered a basic scenario where an integrated solution was created using apps, flows, and bots in a Teams environment and finally moved into another environment for testing or production use.

Summary

In this chapter, we have learned about different types of environments and how they support different life cycle operations that are required for business needs. We also got insights into Power Platform admin center and the administrative capabilities provided by this admin center. This admin center helps us carry out some life cycle operations, such as backup and restore, copy, reset, and delete. These life cycle operations help you to maintain complex scenarios in your organization depending on the business needs.

Similarly, we learned how components such as apps, bots, and flows can be packaged as solutions and migrated between different environments. We also saw the different types of solutions – managed and unmanaged – and why they are needed.

In the next chapter, we will look at how a Dataverse for Teams environment can be upgraded into a full-fledged Microsoft Dataverse environment.

9

Upgrading to Microsoft Dataverse Environment

In the previous chapter, we learned about different types of environments and their associated life cycle operations. We also looked at solutions that help in managing application lifecycles.

In this chapter, we are going to see how to upgrade a **Microsoft Dataverse for Teams Environment** to a standard **Dataverse environment** that can support standalone apps built using **Power Apps**, **Power Automate** flows, and **Power Virtual Agent** bots. Here are the topics that we will cover in this chapter:

- Why upgrade?
- Upgrade process

By the end of this chapter, you will be able to distinguish between a Dataverse for Teams environment and a standard Dataverse environment where you can run standalone apps. You will also have a good understanding of the prerequisites for upgrading from a Dataverse for Teams environment and the upgrade process.

In the following section, we will start by looking at why and when an upgrade might be needed.

Reasons for Upgrading to Microsoft Dataverse

In this section, we will be looking at the scenarios for which an upgrade to a standard Dataverse environment might be needed. There are three reasons why you would consider upgrading a Dataverse for Teams environment into a standard Dataverse environment. These are **Capacity**, **Capabilities**, and **Control**. Let's look at each of these categories and their corresponding details.

Capacity

There are some capacity restrictions while using Dataverse for Teams environments. These restrictions are mainly around the following parameters:

- Number of environments that you are allowed to create within a tenant

- Amount of storage allowed per environment and per tenant (sum of all storage across all environments)

- Number of API requests that a user can make within a 24-hour duration

There are pre-defined values for each of the preceding limits based on the Office family of licenses, and Microsoft has defined them here:

```
https://docs.microsoft.com/en-us/power-platform/admin/about-
teams-environment#capacity-limits
```

These limits are generous enough for you to get started with ample usage and then, once your usage starts hitting any of the limits, you would consider upgrading Dataverse for Teams to a standard Dataverse environment. These limits can change often, so it is best to refer to the latest values provided in the documentation at the link provided.

Let's now look at another factor that would make you consider upgrading – capabilities.

Capabilities

In previous chapters, we have seen that all the **Power Platform** components, such as apps, bots, flows, and tables, had to be built and used within the Microsoft Teams application. In such a Teams environment scenario, some of the Dataverse features are not available. Some features that are not supported are non-relational data, advanced search, and API access. Additionally, there are some advanced security features, such as auditing and activity logging that are not provided with Dataverse for Teams. These capabilities may change over time, so it is better to refer to the list of features and comparisons provided in the Microsoft documentation:

```
https://docs.microsoft.com/en-us/powerapps/teams/data-
platform-compare
```

```
https://docs.microsoft.com/en-us/powerapps/teams/compare-data-
sources
```

These features, or their absence in Dataverse for Teams, is another factor that will require you to consider upgrading your Teams environment.

Licensing

After you upgrade Dataverse for Teams to Dataverse, end users using the apps, flows, and bots will now require having a Power Apps, Power Automate, or Power Virtual Agent apps license. The Office license will no longer be enough to access these components after the upgrade. Please refer to *Chapter 11, Licensing for Microsoft Dataverse and Dataverse for Teams,* for more details on the post-upgrade experience.

Additionally, we need to ensure that there is enough storage capacity within the tenant for an upgrade to take place. This is because after the upgrade the size of the Dataverse for Teams environment (consumption of storage) will accrue storage consumption in the Power Platform tenant-level capacity. Power Platform has strict enforcement rules on storage capacity and, in the absence of enough storage being available, upgrades cannot be started.

Control

As seen in the complete list of features (mentioned in the preceding hyperlink), you will see that there are administration and governance features that will be another factor to consider. The level of control that you get with Dataverse is greater than what you would get with Dataverse for Teams. For example, at the security layer, there is more granular role-based access down to the table and column level. As seen in the following snapshot from a wizard (available during new security role creation), you can see the different options available:

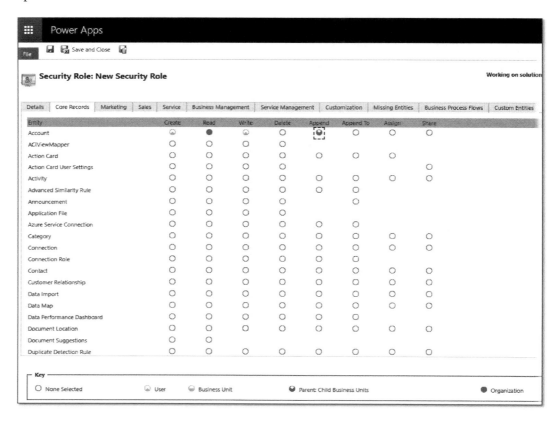

Figure 9.1 – Granular security configuration in Dataverse

You can assign **Create**, **Read**, **Write**, **Delete**, **Append**, **Assign To**, **Assign**, and **Share** privileges to this new role. Besides this, using the **Harvey Ball** UI controls, you can set the level of these privileges – for example, at *User*, *Business Unit*, or *Organization* level. Users who are added to this new security role will be granted permissions within the system based on these privileges and levels. When a level of permission is set at *Business Unit*, the system grants the user access to records in the user's business unit, and when set at `Parent : Child Business Units`, the access is granted to all business units subordinate to the user's business unit. A **Business Unit** is a concept used in Dataverse that helps you logically structure your data and users around departments or divisions within a company or organization that carry out separate functions and business needs. For example, an organization would like to keep its Sales, Customer Service, Human Resources, and Finance divisions separate, and so they will be created as Business Units within Dataverse. When the level is set at *Organization*, the system grants global access to users added to this security role. For a detailed video guide about security in Dataverse, you can view this video:

```
https://www.youtube.com/watch?v=8UWSj-vvxzU
```

Additionally, Dataverse has more advanced encryption features, such as **Customer-Managed Keys** (**CMK**), which allow customers to keep the key to encryption within their **Azure** subscription. This allows customers who use this feature to cut Microsoft's access to this data.

In the next section, we will see how to upgrade a Dataverse for Teams environment into a standard Dataverse environment.

Upgrade Process

In this section, we will walk through the upgrade process, and this process needs to be triggered from the **Power Platform admin center** (**PPAC**). Follow these steps:

1. Navigate to the **Environments** page on PPAC. Here, you will see the different types of environments that are present in this tenant, as seen in the following figure:

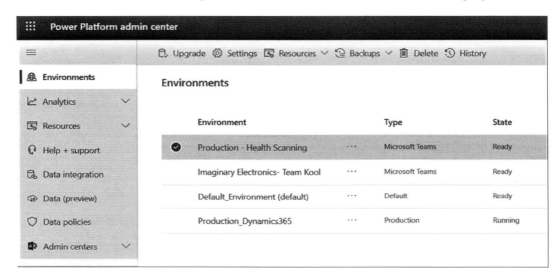

Figure 9.2 – List of different types of environments in PPAC

In the preceding figure, you can see that Dataverse for Teams environments are referred to as **Microsoft Teams** type environments.

2. Select this environment and click the **Upgrade** option on the top menu, as seen in the preceding figure. Clicking this **Upgrade** option will open the upgrade wizard, as seen in the following screenshot:

Figure 9.3 – Launch screen of the upgrade wizard

This launch screen lists the benefits of upgrading, which we discussed in an earlier section – *Reasons for upgrading to Microsoft Dataverse*.

3.   Click the **Next** button on this launch screen and you will see the next screen, which can be seen in the following screenshot. This screen is presented to notify the customers of the impact that this upgrade will have on the users:

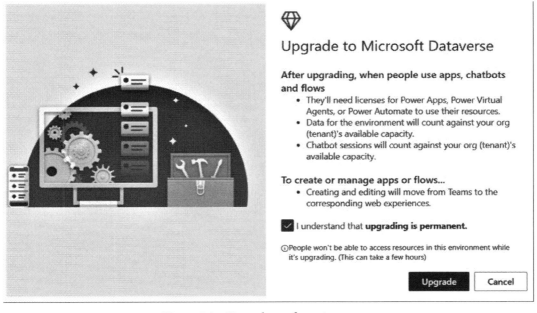

Figure 9.4 – Upgrade confirmation screen

Additionally, this screen also ensures that you acknowledge the fact this upgrade process is irreversible.

> **Important Note**
>
> Once the Dataverse for Teams environment is upgraded to Dataverse, you cannot revert the process and convert the upgraded Dataverse environment back to Dataverse for Teams environment.

4.   Click the **Upgrade** button, as seen in the preceding figure. This will initiate the upgrade process and present a screen showing the status and various stages of the upgrade. The upgrade process is asynchronous and happens in the background:

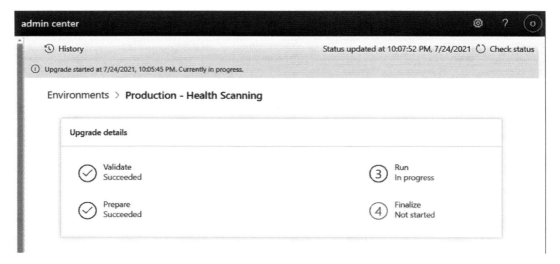

Figure 9.5 – Upgrade in progress

As seen in the following screenshot, there is an option to **Check status** that will fetch the latest status, and the date and time are updated in the **Status updated at <date and time>** message at the top of the screen. This upgrade process may take longer depending on the size of the Teams environment being upgraded.

After the upgrade is completed, you will see the notification that says **Environment was upgraded at <date and time>**, as seen in the following figure:

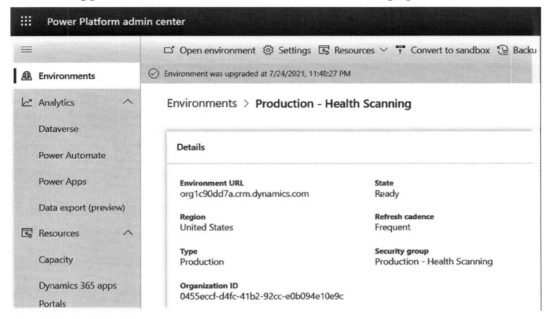

Figure 9.6 – Upgrade completed

5. After the upgrade is completed, let's try to open the **Health Scanner** app from this environment. Click the **Resources drop-down option**, as seen at the top of the screen in the following screenshot:

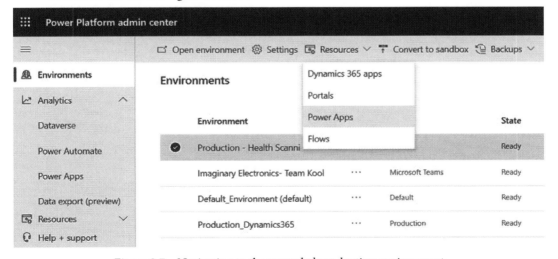

Figure 9.7 – Navigating to the upgraded production environment

6. Select **Power Apps** in the resultant drop-down control, and a new page with all the apps within the newly upgraded environment should be visible. As seen in the following figure, you will see the **Health Scanner** app that we built and migrated to this production environment:

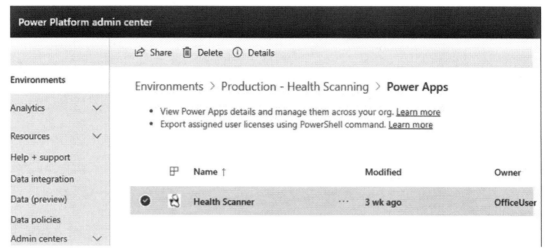

Figure 9.8 – Accessing apps in the newly upgraded environment

7. Click the **Health Scanner** app, and you will see a message on the browser page: **This app uses features that come with a Power Apps premium plan. Start a trial to use these features**:

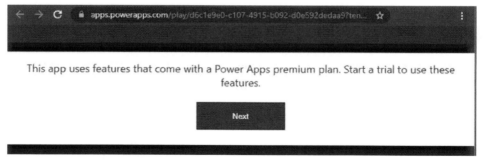

Figure 9.9 – Trial prompt while using apps in the newly upgraded environment

This is because the user (**OfficeUser**) who is accessing this app in the upgraded Dataverse environment now requires a premium license for Power Apps or Power Automate, Power Virtual Agent to access the corresponding components. It is due to these licensing restrictions that warnings were provided before commencing the upgrade process. You can sign up for a trial and continue using this app for a little longer until you procure the appropriate license for this user.

8. Go back to the Microsoft Teams interface and try opening the app, as shown in the following figure. You will see the same licensing error and prompt to start a trial:

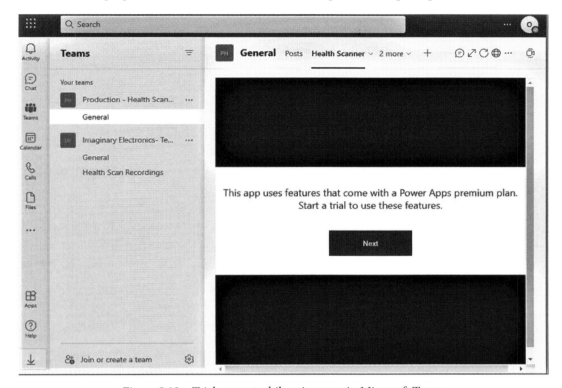

Figure 9.10 – Trial prompt while using apps in Microsoft Teams

We have now seen the complete upgrade process and some of the effects of upgrading on licensing. We will cover more details on the licensing aspects in *Chapter 11, Licensing for Microsoft Dataverse and Dataverse for Teams*.

Summary

In this chapter, we have seen the common reasons for considering an upgrade – capacity, capabilities, and control. We have seen how capacity is limited when using Dataverse for Teams and how some of the capabilities of standard Dataverse, such as the ability to run the apps, bots, and flows outside of Teams, could make you want to upgrade to it. We also learned about the upgrade process and saw each of the steps involved in it. Finally, we were able to see how license restrictions are enforced after the upgrade.

In the next chapter, we will look at security and governance, which are of paramount importance for every organization.

Section 4:
Enterprise Readiness and Licensing

Security is the bedrock of any enterprise application and it is perilous to assume that low-code/no-code applications can ignore this aspect of Application Lifecycle Management. Dataverse for Teams extends the Teams security model to provide good flexibility in terms of different levels of access for different types of audiences, such as team owners and team members. Additionally, there are options to provide guest access to users outside your organization.

Enterprise governance is the practice of setting up policies and processes that ensure that enterprise resources – assets, applications, and systems – are used as per the organization's strategic and/or regulatory compliance needs. Governance policies can be as simple as a naming policy or team/environment creation, but they can be extended for auditing, security, and monitoring usage.

In this section, you will also learn about the licensing aspects of Dataverse for Teams and Dataverse, which will help you understand the different types of licenses and the user entitlements that come with them.

This section comprises the following chapters:

- *Chapter 10, Ensuring Enterprise Readiness: Security and Governance*
- *Chapter 11, Licensing for Microsoft Dataverse and Dataverse for Teams*

10
Ensuring Enterprise Readiness: Security and Governance

In the previous chapter, we learned about scenarios when you would want to consider upgrading a Dataverse for Teams environment to Dataverse. We also covered the steps involved when upgrading and the changes that should be expected for the **user experience (UX)** after an upgrade.

In this chapter, we are going to see some more details about security and governance concepts that are important in a Dataverse for Teams environment. We will also highlight some of the important upgrades to these security and governance areas in Dataverse environments. These are administrative aspects of Dataverse for Teams and hence this chapter is slightly different from the previous chapters, where you were learning to build apps, flows, and bots.

Here are the topics that we will cover in this chapter:

- Implementing a Security Framework in Dataverse for Teams
- Configuring different roles in Dataverse for Teams
- Understanding Governance in Dataverse for Teams

By the end of this chapter, you will have learned about the various security aspects and principles to be applied while using Dataverse for Teams. Additionally, you will have learned about the importance of having governance policies to manage your organization's data and resources.

Let's start with the following section, where we will take a deeper look at the security aspects of Dataverse for Teams.

Implementing a Security Framework in Dataverse for Teams

Security is the bedrock of any enterprise application, and it is perilous to assume that low-code/no-code applications can ignore this aspect of **application lifecycle management** (**ALM**). In this section, we will start with some basic principles of security and look at the various aspects of Dataverse for Teams that help us implement these principles. These basic security principles are outlined here:

- **Confidentiality**—All the data inside an organization should be accessible to only the intended users.
- **Integrity**—Organizational data should not be tampered with by unauthorized users.
- **Availability**—Authorized users should be able to access the data at any time.

To adhere to these principles, different organizations apply various approaches based on the level of awareness and investments needed. However, the bedrock of any such approach would need to have at least these three main strategies:

- Encryption
- Data backups
- Least privilege model

Let's look at each of these strategies in turn.

Encryption

All the data stored in Dataverse for Teams is encrypted at rest (when in storage) and in transit (when data moves between servers within Microsoft data centers). Additionally, all the network traffic (requests and responses) between your computer (browser) to the Microsoft data center, where data is stored in Dataverse for Teams, is encrypted using **Transport Layer Security** (**TLS**). For more information about configuring TLS cipher Suite order, see this link: `https://docs.microsoft.com/en-us/windows-server/security/tls/manage-tls`.

All these encryption measures help to keep bad actors (unauthorized users with malicious intent) from accessing your data through unauthorized means.

Data Backups

Taking frequent backups of the data is another measure that will ensure data integrity can be preserved or restored in the case of corruption or accidental deletion by authorized users. In *Chapter 8, Managing the Application Life Cycle and Environment Life Cycle,* you saw that environment backups are automatically taken by the platform every 10 to 15 minutes. You also learned how you can initiate additional named backups of the environment containing your data using the **Power Platform Admin Center (PPAC)**. These backups can be restored anytime, and hence protect you from data corruption and accidental deletion scenarios. For example, if an authorized user deletes a few records from a Dataverse for Teams table, using the PPAC environment restore functionality can restore a backup of the environment taken just before the deletion. This will restore the deleted records back into the system.

Taking frequent backups of the system helps you to restore the environment in the case of a security issue where a bad actor (an authorized user with malicious intent) deletes some data or if data is deleted accidentally. The platform prevents unauthorized users from accessing any data, so a situation of records being deleted doesn't arise with unauthorized bad actors.

Least privilege model

The least privilege model implies that all users are provided with the least amount of privilege that is required for them. This ensures that unwanted users are kept out of elevated privileges within the system. **Dataverse for Teams** extends the team's security model by providing different levels of access for different types of audiences— **Team Owner** versus **Team Member**. There are also options to add guest users, which is supported by Microsoft Teams.

In this section, we learned about basic security principles and three simple approaches that you can take to secure your business-critical data. In the next section, we will see in detail the different roles provided by Dataverse for Teams and how they help to keep data secure.

Configuring different roles in Dataverse for Teams

In this section, we will see the different types of access that users of Dataverse for Teams can be provided. These types of access depend on **privileges** (the ability to read, write, update, delete, share, and so on) provided to each individual user within the system. Such privileges are grouped together and are known as **roles**.

Understanding standard roles

Let's look at all the out-of-the-box roles provided by Dataverse for Teams.

Owner

A team **owner** role can be compared to that of an administrator. A person assigned an owner role can add/remove new members/guests and change a bunch of team settings, such as controlling member permissions at a very granular layer, creating additional channels under a team, setting the visibility of channels to members, viewing usage of teams and channels, and a lot more. Usually, the person creating a team is by default added as the owner of the team; however, once another owner is added, this can be changed.

From a Dataverse for Teams perspective, owners will have the privilege to perform environment administration tasks such as backup and restore through the PPAC, besides being able to create and run apps, flows, bots, and tables.

Member

As the name suggests, a **member** is part of the team and uses the team for all collaboration activities.

From a Dataverse for Teams perspective, members will have the privilege to create and run apps, flows, bots, and tables within a Dataverse for Teams environment.

Guest

A **guest** is someone outside of your organization who doesn't have a login account with your organization. Typically, these guests are partners, vendors, suppliers, or consultants from companies that do business with your organization.

From a Dataverse for Teams perspective, guests will have the privilege to create and run apps, flows, bots, and tables within a Dataverse for Teams environment. The important difference to note here is that, by default, guests won't have access to data or records created by other members or owners.

The following link shows the capabilities available for each role:

```
https://support.microsoft.com/en-us/office/team-owner-member-
and-guest-capabilities-in-teams-d03fdf5b-1a6e-48e4-8e07-
b13e1350ec7b
```

> **Guest access**
>
> To allow a guest access to collaborate on Microsoft Teams, some configurations need to be done by your admin. For complete details of this step, you can refer to `https://docs.microsoft.com/en-us/microsoftteams/guest-access`.

Adding standard roles to a Dataverse for Teams environment

A new owner, team member, or guest can be added from the Teams **Settings** screen by using the **Add member** button, as seen in the following screenshot:

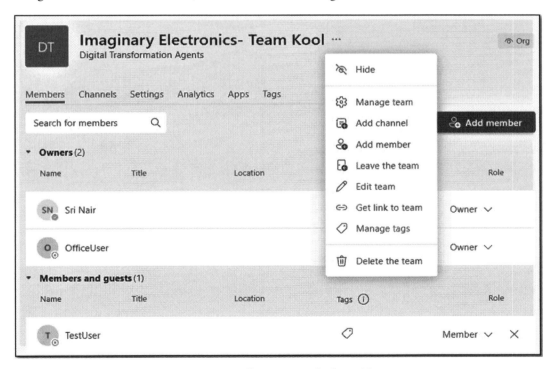

Figure 10.1 – Different types of roles in Teams

The **Manage team** screen can be invoked by clicking the three ellipses dots (...) seen next to the team name.

You can switch roles if you decide to change the role ownership later. This can be done using the drop-down control under **Role** (**Owner/Member**), as shown in the following screenshot:

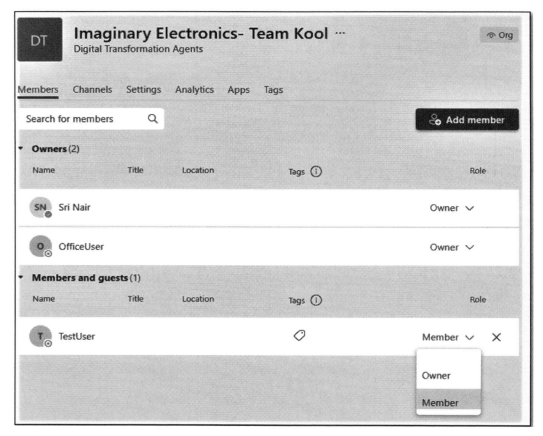

Figure 10.2 – Changing roles in Teams

There are some additional people with privileges present in Dataverse for Teams that are not so obviously visible in Microsoft Teams. We'll talk about them in the next section.

Understanding additional roles in Dataverse for Teams environments

In this section, we are going to look at the following two additional roles in Dataverse for Teams:

- Global admin (Power Platform admin)
- Colleagues with access

Let's take a look at them in more detail.

Global admin (Power Platform admin)

The tenant admins (company- or organization-level admins) who manage all different types of Dataverse environments, including Dataverse for Teams, are also **global admins**. You can imagine this person to be like a super administrator, since these users would have the privilege to perform administrative tasks such as backing up and restoring environments, very much like any owner of a team. These Power Platform admins need not be explicitly added as team owners or members. This privilege comes from the tenant-level role assignment, which is done through the Office administration center (also known as **Microsoft 365 admin center**), as seen in the following screenshot:

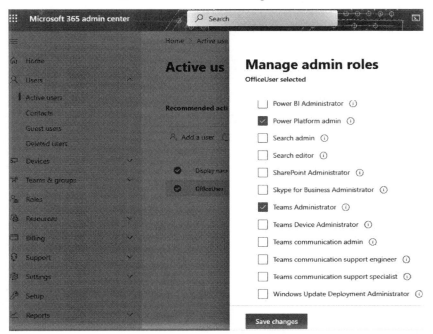

Figure 10.3 – Assigning global admin roles in Teams

Within each Dataverse environment, you will be able to see Power Platform admin users added to a role called **System Administrator**, which we learned about in *Chapter 5, Understanding Microsoft Dataverse*.

Colleagues with access

As the name suggests, quite often there are scenarios where you need to share an app with colleagues who work in the same organization but are not a part of your team. Hence, these colleagues are not added as a member or owner in the Microsoft Teams environment where your team collaborates. Such colleagues, invited to access apps and other data or resources on your team, get added to a role called **Basic User**.

This Basic User role is an out-of-the-box role provided in Dataverse, used for providing privileges to run apps within an environment and perform common actions on Dataverse tables that they own.

In this section, we have seen the different roles that are provided by Dataverse for Teams environments and the various privileges that each of these roles provides. These roles help you to keep your data secure; however, the key underlying action required for this to work is that you provide the least required privilege to users through appropriate roles. It is also essential to carry out an audit of these roles and people added to these roles, on a timely basis. This is because a lot of users change jobs/functions within organizations, and it is important to review and update the privileges of users who are no longer required to have them. Although this would be a primary responsibility of a system administrator to keep data secure, every team member should strive toward this and help by bringing any such change to the administrator's notice at the earliest opportunity.

In the next section, we will look at some of the governance steps that an administrator can take to improve data security.

Understanding Governance in Dataverse for Teams

Today, governance of enterprise resources is of paramount importance, since it enables organizations to swiftly adopt digital transformation while ensuring adequate guardrails are provided to ensure compliance to organization- and industry-level policies. To efficiently govern these resources, policies are crafted and implemented on resources. Governance policies are mostly focused on the areas we will cover in the following sections.

Architecture

Governance of architecture mainly focuses on having an appropriate approach to how data is organized within a tenant—for example, what are the different environment creation policies within the organization? Some organizations will be more particular about the naming convention of environments and default roles and permissions, and so on.

Security

We have already seen some of the best security principles to be followed in the first section, *Implementing a security framework in Dataverse for Teams*. Organizations would like to define a process for requesting access or role assignments. Similarly, Power Platform provides you the ability to prevent data loss by defining policies. Using these policies, an administrator can prevent the loss of critical data from the environment.

Let's look at how configuring a **Data Loss Prevention (DLP)** policy can protect an environment from inadvertent data loss by app makers and users, as follows:

1. Log in to the Power Platform Admin and click on the **Data policies** section, as shown in the following screenshot:

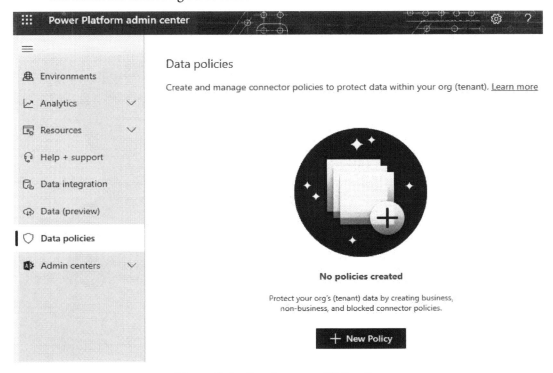

Figure 10.4 – Creating a new DLP policy

2. Next, you will see a wizard-like screen where you can provide a name for your new policy. Let's name this `First_DLP`, as shown in the following screenshot, and click **Next**:

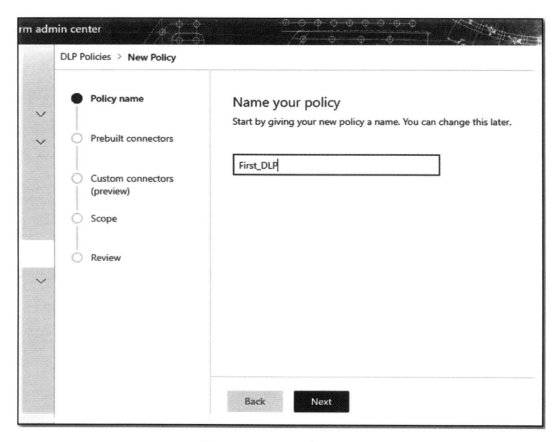

Figure 10.5 – DLP policy name

3. This will load the next screen, which has all the prebuilt connectors, such as **SQL Server**, **Dropbox**, **OneDrive for Business**, and **SharePoint**. We will select the **SQL Server** connector and click **Connector actions** under **Configure connector (preview)**, as illustrated in the following screenshot:

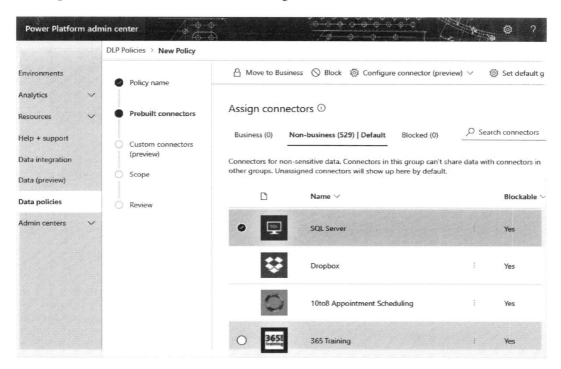

Figure 10.6 – SQL Server Connector actions

Here, you will see that there is an option to block an entire connector with a single button, **Block**. However, for this example, we will continue with blocking selective connector actions to illustrate the granularity at which connector actions can be blocked, using a DLP policy.

4. Clicking **Connector actions** will slide open a new screen on the right that enlists all the SQL Server connector actions, as illustrated in the following screenshot:

Figure 10.7 – DLP policy name

This is the screen where, as an administrator, you will decide which actions of the SQL Server connector need to be blocked. You can block all granular actions supported by the connector. As an administrator, if you don't want anyone to corrupt business-critical data stored across the organization, you will block **Delete row (V2)**, **Insert row (V2)**, **Execute a SQL query (V2)**, **Execute stored procedure (V2)**, **Transform data using Power Query**, and **Update row (V2)**. This can be done by simply changing the toggle under the **Allowed** column to **No**. Similarly, using the **Block new connector actions** radio button, you can block users from writing new actions for this connector.

5. Once you have blocked the allowed actions discussed in the previous step, click **Save**, as shown in the following screenshot:

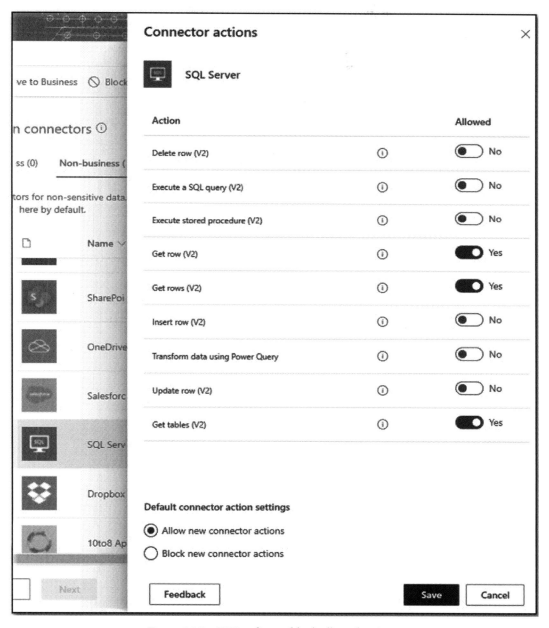

Figure 10.8 – DLP policy to block allowed actions

6. This will take us back to the **Assign Connectors** screen. From there, click **Next** to continue to the next screen of the policy wizard, where you can create additional rules to limit custom connectors.

Clicking the + **Add connector pattern** button at the top of the screen will provide you with options to block **Uniform Resource Locators** (**URLs**) or **application programming interfaces** (**APIs**) for which you don't wish to create custom connectors. Since we don't have any intention to block custom connectors, let's just click the **Next** button to move on, as shown in the following screenshot:

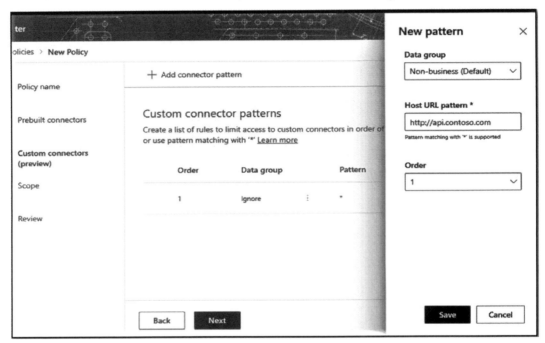

Figure 10.9 – DLP policy to block custom connectors

Custom connectors

While Power Automate provides 300+ connectors to standard data sources, there are situations where you might want to connect to web services provided by data sources that don't have a prebuilt connector. In such cases, Power Automate provides a way to build your own connectors, called custom connectors. You can look at this link if you are interested in building a custom connector: `https://docs.microsoft.com/en-us/connectors/custom-connectors/define-blank`.

7. As seen in the following screenshot, on the **Scope** screen of the wizard, you must decide on the scope of the policy that you are crafting—that is, if you want this new policy being created to be applied to all environments or selective environments, or to exclude any environment:

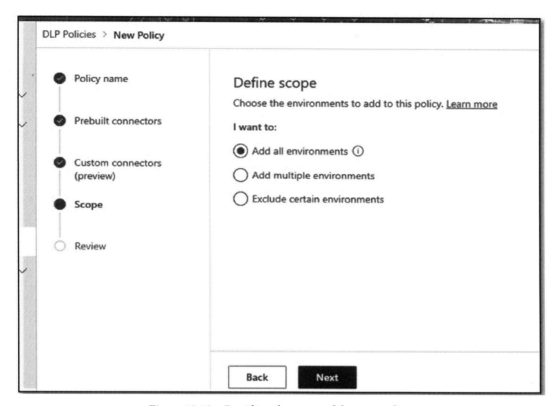

Figure 10.10 – Deciding the scope of the new policy

Depending on your choice on the previous screen—that is, if you chose **Add multiple environments** or **Exclude certain environments**—the next screen will present a list of environments to choose from.

For our illustration, let's keep **Add all environments** and click **Next**. This presents the summary page, which summarizes the choices we made, and then finally, an option to create a policy through the **Create policy** button, as illustrated in the following screenshot:

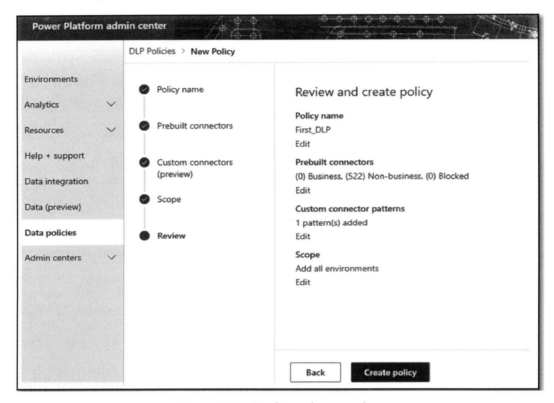

Figure 10.11 – Finalizing the new policy

Clicking this **Create policy** button will complete the policy creation and take you to the home page of **Data policies**, where you will be able to see this newly created `First_DLP` policy, as illustrated in the following screenshot:

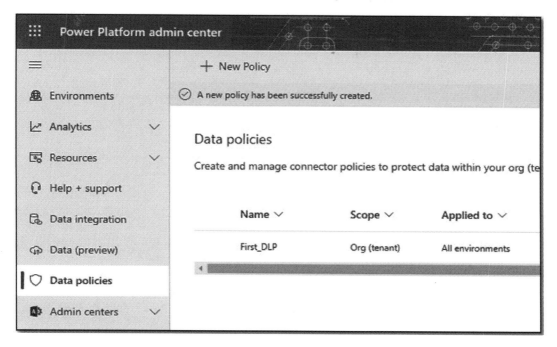

Figure 10.12 – New policy created

You will also see an option to delete this policy, once you select it; you can click this if you wish to delete it in the future.

Auditing or Monitoring

As mentioned in the *Implementing a Security Framework in Dataverse for Teams* section earlier in this chapter, it is important to audit role memberships to ensure that only members who continue to need access are added to each role. Similarly, all activities in Dataverse and apps can be enabled for auditing, to audit changes that happened on those resources and ascertain whether those changes were made by authorized users.

Activity logging and auditing

You can learn about how to enable activity logging for various resources at these links:

Power Apps: `https://docs.microsoft.com/en-us/power-platform/admin/logging-powerapps`

Power Automate: `https://docs.microsoft.com/en-us/power-platform/admin/logging-power-automate`

Dataverse: `https://docs.microsoft.com/en-us/power-platform/admin/enable-use-comprehensive-auditing`

From the preceding links on activity logging, you can see that all activity-logging data is made available in the **Microsoft 365 compliance center** (`https://docs.microsoft.com/en-us/microsoft-365/compliance/microsoft-365-compliance-center?view=o365-worldwide`). Microsoft 365 is a central place that provides access to activity-logging data and helps you manage the compliance needs of your organization.

Monitoring and auditing may also include reviewing app usage from a licensing perspective. For example, are all users of the systems licensed appropriately, or are the licenses utilized efficiently? Are there users with licenses that are no longer needed by them? Such licenses can be reclaimed and reused for other users who need them.

There are some additional licensing entitlement limits which need to be governed. We will cover these licensing entitlement aspects of Dataverse for Teams in the next chapter, *Chapter 11, Licensing for Microsoft Dataverse and Dataverse for Teams*.

Actions based on Auditing or Monitoring

Once auditing and activity logging is monitored, you need to act immediately if an undesired activity is observed. In such cases, Power Automate can help by listening to such triggers through webhooks provided by Microsoft 365 security and compliance services. These triggers can then alert administrators through emails, text messages, or various other mechanisms, as the next step of flows using the several options for connectors that are provided.

Here is a link to complete a step-by-step guide on how you can automate governance activities by taking advantage of the Office 365 Management API and Power Automate flows by connecting to the Microsoft 365 compliance center:

```
https://preview.flow.microsoft.com/en-us/blog/automate-flow-
governance/
```

Thus, we have seen how important it is to have a governance framework and a strategic plan to implement this framework while dealing with business-critical data.

Summary

In this chapter, we have learned about some important aspects of security, such as data protection through the least privilege model, and how Dataverse for Teams helps you implement it using roles. We looked at the different types of roles available within Dataverse for Teams, such as Owner, Member, Guest, Global Admin, and Colleagues with access. We also learned about how data security is provided by the platform through regular backups and encryption. Besides this, we learned how to create a new policy that will help administrators to prevent data loss by blocking certain connectors to critical data sources or specific connector actions. Finally, we saw how governance frameworks can be created and implemented within Dataverse for Teams.

In the next chapter, we will learn about the licensing aspects of Dataverse and Dataverse for Teams, which will help you understand the different types of licenses and the user entitlements that come alongside them.

11
Licensing for Microsoft Dataverse and Dataverse for Teams

In the previous chapter, we learned about key elements of enterprise readiness – security and governance. We also looked at different governance principles and security configurations such as roles and privileges that help you to secure your data within Microsoft Dataverse for Teams.

In this chapter, we will be looking at various licensing aspects that you need to understand while interacting with Microsoft Dataverse for Teams and Microsoft Dataverse. This chapter can also be used as a general reference for the licensing aspects of Power Platform before you make purchasing decisions for your organization.

Here are the topics that we will cover in this chapter:

- Licensing for Power Platform
- Licensing for Microsoft Dataverse for Teams
- Licensing after upgrading to Microsoft Dataverse

By the end of this chapter, you will know about the various aspects and principles used by Microsoft for licensing Power Platform products, including Dataverse for Teams.

Let's start with the first section to get an overview of the licensing needs for Power Platform.

Licensing for Power Platform

In this section, we will look at some of the underlying principles that are used to determine the licensing requirements for Power Platform products. We saw in the initial chapters of this book that Power Platform is a suite of products, including Power BI, Power Apps, Power Automate, Power Virtual Agents, Power Apps portals, and Microsoft Dataverse. The capabilities of these products are seeded either in full or through some features in various other Microsoft product families, such as Office 365, Microsoft 365, and **Dynamics 365**. Dynamics 365 is a suite of CRM applications (for things such as sales, marketing, and customer service) and ERP applications (for things such as finance, supply chain management, and inventory management). As a result of this, you will see the features of Power Platform tiered across Microsoft 365, Power Platform, and Dynamics 365.

Office 365 versus Microsoft 365

Office 365 is a suite of productivity apps and services including Outlook, Word, Excel, and more while Microsoft 365 is a productivity cloud that delivers intelligent experiences, enterprise-grade management, and advanced security to take your business further. Microsoft 365 contains all of the Office 365 features and you can use this link to compare the differences between them: `https://www.microsoft.com/en-us/microsoft-365/ enterprise/compare-microsoft-365-and-office-365`.

Power Platform features exist in both these subfamilies of Office 365 and Microsoft 365; hence, you will see them being used interchangeably within this chapter and book. For simplicity, Microsoft 365 is used throughout this chapter to refer to both Microsoft 365 and Office 365, unless stated otherwise.

The following figure will help you visualize the key features across different product suites:

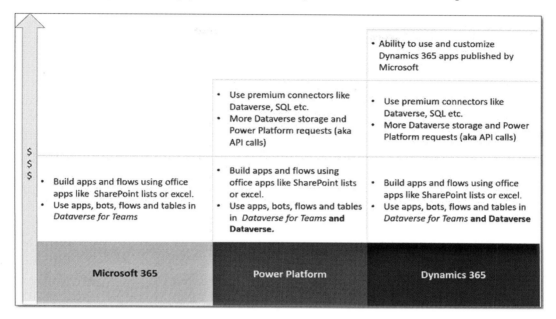

Figure 11.1 – Licensing features across different product suites

In the preceding figure, you can see that the number of features included with each license increases, as we navigate through the product suites from left to right, and understandably the license unit cost (per user) increases accordingly. The license costs differ based on geography and channel (for instance, enterprise sector, small or medium business, educational sector, or non-profit). Also, the list of features shown in the preceding figure is not exhaustive but rather is a good subset to illustrate the major differences between the features available in various product suites. Since product licensing is an evolving area, refer to the product licensing guide for the latest complete list of features. The latest licensing guide for Power Platform can be found at this link: `https://powerapps.microsoft.com/en-us/pricing/`. As a general principle in licensing for Power Platform, licensing for end users is needed only when using a Power Platform component, for example, when using an app, invoking a flow, or using a bot. The following users/scenarios are exempted from requiring a license:

1. Administration scenarios such as using features inside the **Power Platform admin center** (**PPAC**). As seen in the previous chapter, *Chapter 10, Ensuring Enterprise Readiness: Security and Governance*, administration scenarios are considered essential operations to keep your data safe and secure and hence they are excluded from being considered something for which a product license is needed.

2. Making or creating an app, flow, or bot and extending the customization of an existing app are scenarios that don't require a license.

Based on the preceding principles, it is now obvious that there is no cost for making or customizing Power Platform artifacts such as apps, bots, and flows, and the cost of licensing is directly proportional to the number of end users who will be using the apps, bots, and flows that are built. So, it is evident that any organization or developer would want to evaluate the product and get some hands-on validation of or training on the features available, before planning for investment in procuring the licenses. Power Platform helps developers and organizations to try out these features for free, either for a limited audience as in the case of a developer instance or for a limited time, as in the case of a trial instance.

Free Tier

Power Platform provides a free tier through the Power Apps trial subscription with the Microsoft 365 Developer Program – at no cost. Details on how to get one of these subscriptions are available at `https://developer.microsoft.com/en-us/microsoft-365/dev-program`.

Figure 11.2 – Joining the Microsoft 365 Developer Program

Clicking on the **Join now** button, as seen in the preceding figure, will prompt you to sign up with a Microsoft account. If you do not have a Microsoft account, you can create one using this site: `https://account.microsoft.com/account`.

Similarly, you can also sign up for a Power Apps trial (for a limited duration) at this site: `https://powerapps.microsoft.com/`.

Now that we have an overview of the different product suites and a high-level view of the features from Power Platform available within these product suites, let's look at the licensing requirements for Microsoft Dataverse for Teams.

Licensing for Microsoft Dataverse for Teams

Microsoft Dataverse for Teams is part of the offering that comes with the Office license, now known as Microsoft 365. As illustrated in *Figure 11.1*, with the Microsoft 365 license, you can build apps, flows, and bots while using other Office products such as SharePoint lists or Excel as the data storage option. These apps, bots, and flows will be able to run standalone; that is, you can run or invoke them separately in their own player or browser as needed. However, when you modify an app to add a Dataverse connector and then run it, it would trigger a license check failure. That is, you will be prompted to get a separate Power Apps, Power Automate, or Power Virtual Agents license. However, if you wish to just use Dataverse for Teams and not Dataverse, as seen through all the chapters in this book, you can continue building and using such apps, bots, and flows with your Microsoft 365 license.

Similarly, these apps, flows, and bots that are built in Dataverse for Teams cannot be run outside of Teams. For example, if you open the maker portal (`https://make.powerapps.com`) and try to find these apps or try to navigate to your Dataverse for Teams environment, you won't be able to find these options.

Hence, Microsoft Dataverse for Teams can be used by users with Microsoft 365 licenses.

As of the time of writing, here are the Microsoft 365 licenses with which you will be able to use Dataverse for Teams:

- Office 365 E1, E3, E5

- Microsoft 365 E1, E3, E5

- Microsoft 365 F1, F3, F5

The differences between the E1, E3, and E5 plans for Office 365 can be viewed here: `https://www.microsoft.com/en-us/microsoft-365/enterprise/compare-office-365-plans`, while the differences between the Microsoft 365 plans (E1, E3, and E5) can be found here: `https://www.microsoft.com/en-us/microsoft-365/compare-microsoft-365-enterprise-plans`.

Similarly, the different plans for frontline workers (referred to as the F1, F3, and F5 plans) can be found here: `https://www.microsoft.com/en-us/microsoft-365/enterprise/frontline#office-SKUChooser-0dbn8nt`.

You will see in these different plans that all Microsoft 365 and Office 365 plans have Power Platform features listed under **Work management**. Also, they are mentioned as partially included, referring to the missing premium features such as the ability to use premium connectors such as Dataverse. However, you will observe that Microsoft Teams (listed under **Meetings and voice**) is included completely. This allows Dataverse for Teams to be available for users with all Office 365 and Microsoft 365 plans.

In the next section, we will focus on the specific impact of licensing after Dataverse for Teams is upgraded to Microsoft Dataverse.

Licensing after upgrading to Microsoft Dataverse

In *Chapter 9, Upgrading to Microsoft Dataverse Environment*, we saw the reasons to consider upgrading a Dataverse for Teams environment to Dataverse. These reasons or features were around greater capacity, better capabilities, and more control over security and administration. We also saw how the upgrade process can be initiated from the PPAC and briefly touched upon the after effects of upgrading. As seen in the following figure, after upgrading, the app that was working from Teams can now not be launched:

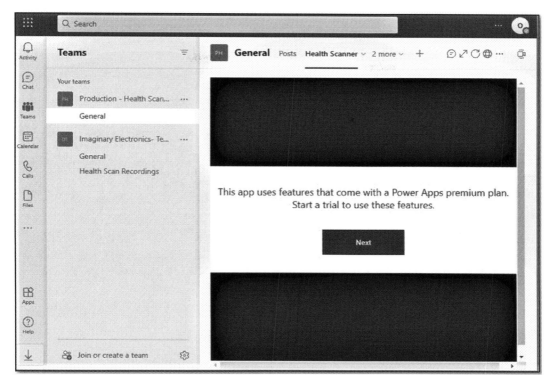

Figure 11.3 – App cannot launch after upgrading to Dataverse

As seen in the error message, this app uses features that come with the Power Apps premium plan; that is, this app is now connected to an upgraded Dataverse instance, instead of Dataverse for Teams. As seen in *Figure 11.1*, connecting to Dataverse, or using a Dataverse connector, requires the end user to have a Power Apps license.

In this scenario with Health Scanner, once we upgrade the Dataverse for Teams instance to Dataverse, all users of Health Scanner will now be required to have a Power Apps license.

We also saw how the end users weren't able to launch the same app in a browser outside the Teams application. Before upgrading, it was not possible due to feature and navigation restrictions; however, after upgrading, a user with a Microsoft 365 license can launch it from the PPAC, but you will see a similar licensing error, as shown in the following screenshot:

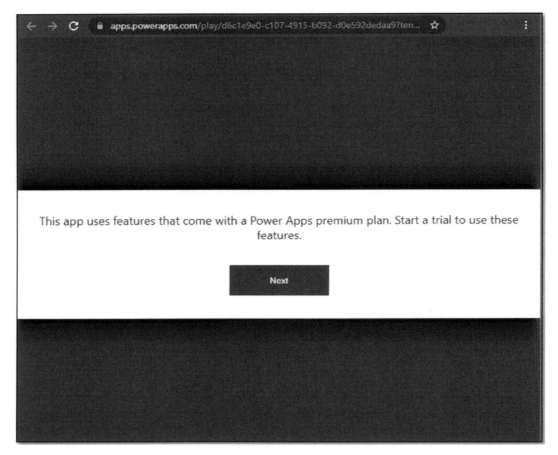

Figure 11.4 – Trial prompt while using Power Apps in the newly upgraded environment

However, once you have acquired a Power Apps license for the end users and assigned it through the Microsoft 365 admin center, these end users can navigate to Health Scanner and start using it, as seen in the following screenshot:

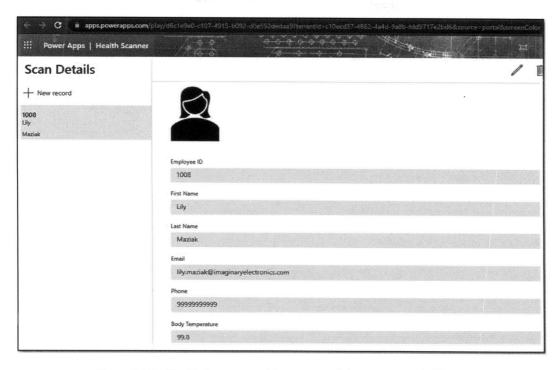

Figure 11.5 – Health Scanner working as a standalone app outside Teams

Similarly, flows and Power Virtual Agents can be launched independently, outside of the Teams application, as seen in the following screenshot of a Health Scanner bot being launched as an independent bot within the browser, outside the Teams application:

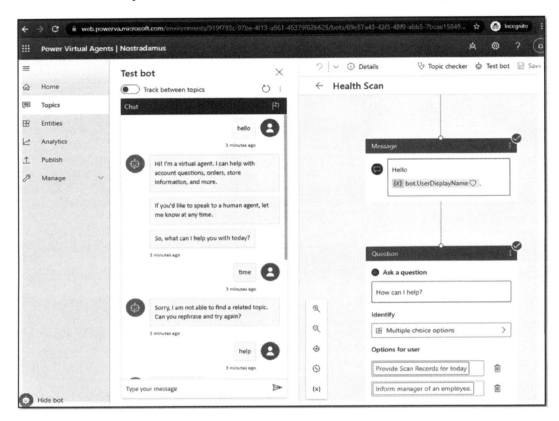

Figure 11.6 – Power Virtual Agents bot working as a standalone bot outside Teams

Additionally, once Dataverse for Teams is upgraded to Dataverse, the following feature categories are where you will see increased features or capabilities that can be leveraged to make the Health Scanner application more refined and robust.

Environment and Application Life Cycle

After upgrading to Dataverse, the environment has all the abilities to promote the schema further, which can be leveraged to run Dynamics 365 business applications. Environment life cycle operations such as resetting or copying an environment are now possible with an upgraded environment. Applications can be packaged as managed or unmanaged solutions, thus helping with better **Application life cycle management** (**ALM**).

Capacity Entitlements

Dataverse storage and Power Platform request entitlements are increased, meaning an application can store more records and carry out more transactions before hitting any capacity limits.

Client Access

With an upgraded Dataverse instance, data can be accessed from Teams, a web browser, a mobile player, or any other application that can connect to data, such as Excel or Power BI.

Data Options

Besides advanced datatypes (email, phone, URL, and so on), Dataverse also provides options for non-relational data and managed data lakes, search capabilities on this data, and mobile offline features. With intelligent search out of the box, you can find insights from your data without needing to build your own search engine or using external AI solutions to derive insights. The mobile offline feature allows users to interact with data on mobile devices in offline mode without an internet connection, which helps end users to stay productive in situations of low or no connectivity to the internet.

Advanced Security

Even though Dataverse for Teams provides data encryption and role-based security, Dataverse supports advanced security configurations such as customer-managed keys, field-level security, and auditing features.

Data integration and Reporting

With Dataverse, you can leverage the **Data Export Service (DES)**, which helps customers to replicate data to Microsoft Azure SQL Database in a customer-managed Azure subscription. More details about the DES can be found here: `https://docs.microsoft.com/en-us/powerapps/developer/data-platform/data-export-service`.

Additionally, for exporting data from Dataverse to Azure Data Lake Storage Gen2, you can leverage **Azure Synapse Link**. You will find more details on Azure Synapse Link for Dataverse at this link: `https://docs.microsoft.com/en-us/powerapps/maker/data-platform/export-to-data-lake`.

Similarly, you can build rich Power BI reports by connecting to Dataverse or also leverage paginated **SQL Server Report Services (SSRS)** reports with Dataverse.

Pro-Dev features

An **application programming interface (API)** is the key ingredient of a robust platform, and with Dataverse you get all the API support you need, including REST OData, SOAP, and a well-documented **software development kit (SDK)**. If you are a professional developer, then there are a bunch of tools and resources to leverage Dataverse. You can find these tools and resources here: `https://docs.microsoft.com/en-us/powerapps/developer/data-platform/developer-tools`.

We have seen that while there are licensing implications for end users who must use apps, bots, and flows in an upgraded Dataverse environment, there are additional features that will be helpful in your digital transformation journey. Hence, while considering an upgrade to Dataverse, all these aspects must be factored in before deciding to upgrade a Dataverse for Teams environment. It is also important to note that once you have upgraded to Dataverse, the relationship with the Teams environment is broken and there is no way to revert to a Dataverse for Teams environment or link it back to the original Microsoft Teams.

Summary

In this last chapter, we have seen how to evaluate licensing requirements while using different Power Platform products. We also looked at how Power Platform products and features are embedded in other product suites such as Office 365/Microsoft 365 and Dynamics 365, and their corresponding licensing requirements. Finally, we have also seen how upgrading a Dataverse for Teams environment impacts the licensing requirements for end users, while also seeing the advanced features that are available after upgrading to Microsoft Dataverse.

I would like to conclude this chapter by sharing some inspiring stories of individuals who are transforming their careers, lives, and organizations by adopting this low-code/no-code revolution with Power Platform:

- How a school teacher used Power Apps to transform classroom management and motivate students: `https://www.youtube.com/watch?v=Y3YiR3ZOTDc&list=PLi9EhCY4z99XX7IuNzu08__5U6JASdvaL&index=47`.

- How 10-year-old twins turned ideas about rating books and scanning for allergies into reality with Microsoft Power Apps: `https://www.youtube.com/watch?v=meKGuxu7ge0&list=PLi9EhCY4z99XX7IuNzu08__5U6JASdvaL&index=4`.

- How a security officer at Heathrow airport created digital transformation and become an IT professional: `https://www.youtube.com/watch?v=tBc9ophAYCc&list=PLi9EhCY4z99XX7IuNzu08__5U6JASdvaL&index=49`.

There are several such stories that will inspire you to continue this journey of low-code/ no-code development with Power Platform here: `https://www.youtube.com/ playlist?list=PLi9EhCY4z99XX7IuNzu08__5U6JASdvaL`.

As I conclude this book, I would like to congratulate you on starting your citizen development career. I hope that this book sparked enough curiosity for you to embark on this mission of digital transformation within your organization!

Packt.com

Subscribe to our online digital library for full access to over 7,000 books and videos, as well as industry leading tools to help you plan your personal development and advance your career. For more information, please visit our website.

Why subscribe?

- Spend less time learning and more time coding with practical eBooks and Videos from over 4,000 industry professionals

- Improve your learning with Skill Plans built especially for you

- Get a free eBook or video every month

- Fully searchable for easy access to vital information

- Copy and paste, print, and bookmark content

Did you know that Packt offers eBook versions of every book published, with PDF and ePub files available? You can upgrade to the eBook version at packt.com and as a print book customer, you are entitled to a discount on the eBook copy. Get in touch with us at customercare@packtpub.com for more details.

At www.packt.com, you can also read a collection of free technical articles, sign up for a range of free newsletters, and receive exclusive discounts and offers on Packt books and eBooks.

Other Books You May Enjoy

If you enjoyed this book, you may be interested in these other books by Packt:

Empowering Organizations with Power Virtual Agents

Nicolae Tarla

ISBN: 978-1-80107-474-2

- Get to grips with Power Virtual Agents and understand the license requirement for using it
- Deploy bots on public websites or web pages
- Create conversational solutions for your organization using Microsoft Teams
- Explore best practices for governance that are essential for implementing Power Virtual Agents
- Explore different business scenarios for implementing Power Virtual Agents
- Understand the integration between Power Virtual Agents and Microsoft Power Platform

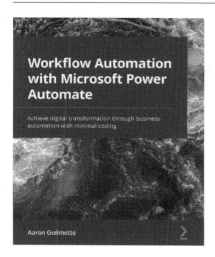

Workflow Automation with Microsoft Power Automate

Aaron Guilmette

ISBN: 978-1-83921-379-3

- Get to grips with the building blocks of Power Automate, its services, and core capabilities

- Explore connectors in Power Automate to automate email workflows

- Discover how to create a flow for copying files between two cloud services

- Understand the business process, connectors, and actions for creating approval flows

- Use flows to save responses submitted to a database through Microsoft Forms

- Find out how to integrate Power Automate with Microsoft Teams

Packt is searching for authors like you

If you're interested in becoming an author for Packt, please visit authors. packtpub.com and apply today. We have worked with thousands of developers and tech professionals, just like you, to help them share their insight with the global tech community. You can make a general application, apply for a specific hot topic that we are recruiting an author for, or submit your own idea.

Hi!

I am Srikumar Nair, author of Digital Transformation with Dataverse for Teams. I really hope you enjoyed reading this book and found it useful in learning about low-code/no-code application development using Microsoft Dataverse for Teams.

It would really help me (and other potential readers!) if you could leave a review on Amazon sharing your thoughts on Digital Transformation with Dataverse for Teams.

Your review will help me to understand what's worked well in this book, and what could be improved upon for future editions, so it really is appreciated.

Best Wishes,

Index

Printed in Great Britain
by Amazon